Not An Accidental Rise

HARSH VARDHAN SHRINGLA

Not An Accidental Rise

HARSH VARDHAN SHRINGLA

DIPMALA ROKA

KNOWLEDGE WORLD

KW Publishers Pvt Ltd
New Delhi

ISBN 978-93-94915-47-3 Hardback
ISBN 978-93-94915-49-7 Paperback
ISBN 978-93-94915-48-0 ebook

Published in India by Kalpana Shukla

KNOWLEDGE WORLD

KW Publishers Pvt Ltd
4676/21, First Floor, Ansari Road
Daryaganj, New Delhi 110002
Phone: +91 11 43528107
Marketing: kw@kwpub.in
Editorial: production@kwpub.in
Website: www.kwpub.in

Printed and Bound in India

CONTENTS

AUTHOR'S NOTE

I FIRST MET Mr. Harsh Vardhan Shringla on April 3, 2021. This was when he visited Gangtok for the IVth Global Lecture Series organised by the Department of International Relations, Sikkim University.

Since my department was organising the lecture, I was fortunate to interact with him and was fascinated by what he appeared to represent. He belonged to my region and had risen to one of the highest positions that an Indian civil servant could hold. I was aware that he came from a respected and well-known family from Darjeeling with a Sikkimese connection.

But when he began his presentation in Nepali, everyone was ecstatic and pleased. Hearts were bursting with pride. We came to understand that despite being a global citizen who had represented India at the major diplomatic capitals of the world, he was still very much one of us. It was clear that he felt a deep and strong connection, affinity, and compassion for the land of his ancestors.

He delivered an insightful lecture that came from deep understanding and reflection regarding the nature and content of the foreign policy. What impressed me, even more, was his humility. He wore his position lightly and was remarkably open and accessible. He was eager to interact with students and youth. I was fortunate to spend some time with him during his visit to Sikkim University, which gave me inspiration for this book. This book is a sincere attempt to capture Harsh Vardhan Shringla as a person and a diplomat who could inspire the youth to become achievers.

I worked closely with him while writing this book, and this gave me insights into the making of India's foreign policy that no amount of academic work could provide. The first-hand account from a senior diplomat who has extensively dealt with some of the contemporary major global challenges was immensely enlightening. It made a deep impression on me, and I hope that it will leave an enduring mark on those who read this book.

Writing this book gave me an opportunity to get to know him as a person. I was able to see beneath the exterior, and I saw in him a true human being who was always giving to others and did so without any expectation of return.

He is a self-made man who has risen by dint of sheer grit and hard work. His perseverance and determination are remarkable, as are his skills as a diplomat and an administrator. He innovates constantly.

A true son of India Harsh Vardhan Shringla, believes in the glorious destiny of our nation and is determined and committed to doing everything to help our nation achieve its goals because he truly believes in its future. He has made every effort to accurately reflect this India with the utmost sincerity and to the best of his ability, knowledge, and skill.

Dipmala Roka

Gangtok, March 9, 2023

ACKNOWLEDGEMENTS

WRITING A book is a team effort, and I am grateful for the support and encouragement of many people along the way.

First and foremost, I would like to thank all of those who I have interviewed for sharing their personal impressions of Mr. Harsh Vardhan Shringla. He has made friends wherever he has gone, and these friends gave freely of their valuable time.

Harsh Shringla inspires loyalty and respect amongst his colleagues. Several officers who have served with him during his long and distinguished career gave valuable input and shared recollections. I express my gratitude to Dr. Anupam Ray—who has reluctantly agreed to be acknowledged, for his support and encouragement. His advice and knowledge were crucial in helping to shape this work into its final form.

I would also like to extend my heartfelt thanks to Dr. B. Bala Bhaskar who provided feedback and insights. His constructive criticism helped me refine my ideas and improve the quality of the final product. My thanks to

Shishir Kothari and Norden for their extensive support. I am grateful for the help I received from Renu Mann and Shreepath.

I would like to thank the members of the extended Shringla family in multiple locations across the world for the information they shared. It remains, despite being very dispersed and close-knit, with strong family values and an enduring sense of identity.

I acknowledge the information placed in the public domain by the Ministry of External Affairs and on social media by the Indian Diplomatic Mission, which I have accessed.

I express my thanks to Kalpana Shukla who patiently bore with my delays.

I am grateful to Ama and Baba, and my sisters Deepshikha and Deeprekha, for their unconditional support. I also acknowledge the support of my family and friends, especially my husband, Mr. Sanjeeb Lama, who provided endless encouragement and patience throughout the writing process. I would also like to mention my nephews Devansh, Danish and Sriansh for bringing joy into my life.

Last but not the least, I express my heartfelt gratitude to Mr. Harsh Vardhan Shringla for believing in me and giving me this once in a lifetime opportunity. I will remain forever grateful.

I would like to express my appreciation to the readers who will take the time to read this book. Your interest and support make it worthwhile.

Dipmala Roka
Gangtok, March 9, 2023

PREFACE

INDIA IS a land of many cultures, languages, and religions. It is a civilisation that synthesises these influences into a composite whole that is greater than its parts. It does so despite being vast and diverse, and despite major social, economic, and developmental challenges. There are many reasons for its resilience and—some might say—its surprising success.

Harsh Vardhan Shringla's life and career are powerful examples of this Indian story. It is a story of how a man who is deeply connected to his roots and his heritage rose by virtue of sheer character and ability to one of the highest positions in the land. It is an account of grit and hard work, perseverance, determination, and skill. It is a tale of how this son of Darjeeling and Sikkim was entrusted with great responsibilities and represented India on the world stage, and eventually rose to the highest position in the elite Indian Foreign Service.

Harsh Shringla has roots in Darjeeling and Sikkim, his family is well known for a long record of public service. He has not risen by accident, though he had the advantage of far-sighted parents who worked single-mindedly to ensure a brighter future for their children. He has, however, lived in and been exposed to different parts of the country. His father's postings in Mumbai (twice), Chennai, Kolkata, Delhi and Ahmedabad took him to these places. He was schooled in Rajasthan and went to University in Delhi.

He inherited an extremely strong work ethic from his parents and always felt that it was preferable to gain work experience than seek higher degrees. He went straight to work after graduation—first in the private sector, and then in the public sector—before joining the Indian Foreign Service at the relatively young age of 22.

He has had an unusually distinguished career and was always entrusted with key responsibilities in virtually all major geographical areas in which the Ministry of External Affairs operates. He began his career by undergoing language training in Paris where, in accordance with the requirements of the service, he learned the French language. He was then moved to East Asia with a posting in Vietnam. When he returned to the Ministry's Headquarters, he was deployed in the Europe West Division that oversaw India's relations with major European countries, and was then promoted and moved to the Northern Division. The Northern Division covers India's relations with Nepal and Bhutan and is considered to be one of the "heaviest" territorial units in the Ministry. His next posting in Tel Aviv meant working on India's relations with Israel and understanding the complicated politics of the Middle East and the Islamic world. From Tel Aviv, Shringla moved to the United Nations and the world of multilateral diplomacy when he was appointed to the Permanent Mission of India to the United Nations at New York. Many consider this to be India's flagship mission which attracts the best and brightest amongst IFS officers. His next assignment as Consul General of India in Durban gave him working experience in the emerging continent of Africa.

He returned thereafter to his longest stint at Headquarters as Joint Secretary in the Ministry of External Affairs. While working at this key operating level he successively managed the SAARC, UN Political, and BSM (Bangladesh, Sri Lanka, Myanmar and Maldives) Divisions.

His joining the IFS at a relatively young age meant that he was entrusted with responsibilities that were unusually heavy for his age. For example, he became Consul General in Ho Chi Minh City at the age of 26. This meant that he opened a Consulate General, and established an Indian presence in that part of Vietnam, while still in his twenties. This allowed him to build up an extremely diverse professional "portfolio" with insight and experience in virtually all of India's major diplomatic accounts. He has worked in Embassies, High Commissions, and Consulates and has worked in North America, Europe, Africa, the Middle East, South Asia, South East Asia, and East Asia. His extensive experience of the neighbourhood is important and crucial in the era of Neighbourhood First diplomacy. He has both bilateral and multilateral experience and has worked on key political accounts. His record in economic diplomacy includes traditional trade and investment promotion as well as a rich and substantial developmental partnership exposure in the neighbourhood.

He has been Consul General in Durban—in addition to Ho Chi Minh City—Ambassador of India to Thailand, High Commissioner of India in Bangladesh, and was Ambassador of India to the United States before being appointed Foreign Secretary. This is the trajectory of an officer who earned his way to every position that he has occupied. It is not an accidental rise. It is the story of each promotion being built on the achievements of the last.

Through all this, Harsh Shringla remains, according to the people whom I have interviewed, a deeply humble and grounded man. He is popular amongst his colleagues. He is soft-spoken and courteous to a fault. He has a reputation for being a leader, a man who works shoulder-to-shoulder with his team. His seniors have relied upon him, and his juniors respect him and look up to him. His human qualities have endeared him to the "other ranks" in the Ministry. His personal staff and his subordinates, often the best judge of an officer's character, have always liked working for him. He is also popular amongst his batchmates and contemporaries. Stories abound amongst those who have worked for him for his sympathy and understanding and for his consideration of their professional and personal requirements.

Through all this, Harsh Shringla also remains a son of the soil. He is deeply connected to the land of his ancestors, to his immediate and extended family. He has been concerned about giving back to his state and the region to which he and his ancestors belong. Shringla is a born leader and a person with deeply human qualities. He has worked his way through the ranks to his current elevated status and position. It is difficult to argue against the idea that he might have been one of the best-prepared persons—by virtue of his record and experience—to hold the position of Foreign Secretary.

1

EARLY DAYS AND FAMILY

HARSH VARDHAN SHRINGLA was born in Mumbai on May 1, 1962 to Tshering Tendup La, popularly known as T. T. La, and Hari Devi Basnet (Chhetri). Although he was born in Mumbai and had the opportunity to live in different parts of the country, Shringla has roots in Darjeeling and Sikkim as both of his parents are from Darjeeling and spoke Nepali at home. There has often been speculation about his family name Shringla. Many mistake it for the North Indian name of Singla. His name derives from the Tibetan word Tshering-la. His great-grandfather wrote his name as Sharab Shringla, and that tradition has been continued by Shringla and his brother, Suberna Shringla. There is now a new generation of Shringlas; his closest cousin (Lulu) was also named Sharab Shringla after his great-grandfather.

Darjeeling has always been home for the Shringlas who also have strong connections to Sikkim. Geographically, Sikkim and Darjeeling are adjacent to each other as they are part of the same Himalayan range over which the mighty Kanchenjunga towers. The Teesta and Rangeet rivers flow from this beautiful area and unite in the Triveni which can be approached from Darjeeling and from Gangtok. These two towns, and Siliguri, are the main reference points in that area.

Harsh Shringla's paternal family was locally prominent in the area of public service and business. His family made every effort to give direction based on strong values and a sense of responsibility to its young. Bonds in the family, and in the extended family, as is expected in Nepali-Bhutia cultural milieu, are durable. He was a devoted son to his parents and tended to his father in his last days despite being occupied by a busy schedule at work. Harsh Shringla was greatly inspired by his father's deep convictions on anything that he would do. His father not only helped people around him, but also taught these virtues to his two sons.

His father believed in providing the best education and opportunities for his children. At the same time, he was realistic enough to know that he needed to prepare them for a challenging, competitive and somewhat unsympathetic environment ahead. His father was never one to accept failure in himself or his children. Harsh Shringla recounts an incident when he returned home crying after a physical fight with a bigger boy. Contrary to his expectation, his father had no sympathy for him. He simply said, "go fight it out". At the same time, he recalls the warmth of his feelings when his father came through for him time and again when he needed him most. When advised by friends to withdraw him from boarding school when he was not performing in the early days in a new environment, his father allowed him to continue, saying "I have faith in him." Emerging after a hard day at junior school or seeing his father drive up in the family car to pick him up and his schoolmates after a trip to the zoo were enduring memories for him.

Harsh Shringla's father always encouraged him to join the Indian Foreign Service. His father was of the generation that began their careers in the years after independence, and he urged his children to serve their country. To that generation, there could be no greater honour than to represent India. He also believed that there was nothing more significant than representing India—at a time when Sikkim had become the latest State of the Union of India—and to helping people in whatever manner one could. His father's work ethic and determination had a strong effect on his son. Shringla, at an early stage in life, decided that he wanted to join the Indian Foreign Service.

His parents, like him, were family-oriented and passed it on as heritage. Equal emphasis was placed on modern education and traditional culture. Shringla had a cosmopolitan upbringing and went to boarding school and college in North India. His early education in various parts of India made him grasp the diversity of India, exposed him to the rich and varied cultures of India's food and traditions, and contributed to his pan-India outlook. The deep roots of his native place, however, continued to shape his personality. He regularly visited his close relatives and family friends which kept him deeply entrenched emotionally.

Harsh Shringla's grandfather was an astute and successful businessman. He built his business to take advantage of the limited commercial opportunities in Darjeeling at a time of colonial rule and domination. He established businesses that catered to the British needs of the time. He supplied the schools and all other institutions, including the Darjeeling jail, with their provisions, ranging from processed food items to fruits and vegetables. Sharab Lama & Sons were officially appointed Purveyors to His Majesty's Government. The extended family—all Sikkimese of Buddhist descent—also did very well. Sharab Lama's brother, Tenduf La was the proprietor of what continues to be one of the most famous hotels in Darjeeling. Windamere Hotel, which occupies the town's best location on Observatory Hill. His aunt was married into the reputed Ladenla family.

Darjeeling was established as a hill station by the British to escape the heat and humidity of Calcutta in the summer months. Schools, colleges, the race course, the Mall, and the famous Darjeeling Himalayan Railway (known as the toy train) were British creations for their own interests. Later, tea was introduced into the mix, and Darjeeling became famous for its 3 Ts—Tea, Tourism, and the Toy Train. However, the family failed to adjust to changing times in post-independent India and the business faltered. As the youngest son, Shringla's father did not wait to be accommodated in the family business. He completed his MA in Economics from Calcutta University and was selected for a Class I post in the Forward Markets Commission in Mumbai. He went on to become Joint Director General of Foreign Trade in the Government of India.

Harsh Shringla himself had the opportunity to integrate more into mainstream India than his parents in their childhood or others from his family. His father wanted to give him the best possible education. He chose a residential school to insulate him and his brother, Suberna from an itinerant existence of a transferable job. As a result, Shringla was schooled at Mayo College in Ajmer and went on to get his Bachelor's degree from St. Stephen's College, Delhi.

Harsh Shringla has never really lived in Darjeeling but the strength of the bonds that he has with family and the region is evident in the connection that he retains with his close relatives and friends, distance and time have not dimmed them.

His brother, Suberna, is a successful management and finance professional who has built his career in Hong Kong and Singapore. The brothers remained extremely close, conversing regularly even while Shringla held very demanding jobs that kept him busy. The forty years that they have spent apart have, according to his brother, produced a relationship in which there is genuine love and respect. Conversations between them are low on words but the deep affection and regard that they have for each other is apparent. Suberna Shringla remembers a brother who was outwardly stern but was a pillar of strength and support in Mayo College, where he followed his sibling. When a young Suberna, still in the middle house in school, was bullied, he turned to his brother. He remembers, gratefully, that his brother who was already in the senior house, and an influential student, intervened to set things right. A part of the strong bond between the brothers, and the younger brother's obvious admiration for the elder, go back to the older brother looking out for his younger sibling in school.

His cousin, Neena Khadka, however, remembers him as a more sentimental person. Neena's father and Harsh Shringla's mother were siblings, she remembers a childhood in which the entire family spent a considerable amount of time together. She says that Shringla was always protective of his younger brother, Suberna. She has a distinct recollection of the brothers crying when Shringla went to boarding school. She recalled how Harsh Shringla, known as Harshoo in the family, was nurtured as a much loved child but, at the same time, with a strong emphasis on his education and all-round personality development. Appreciating his interest in the violin, his parents took special care to take him to violin classes.

Harsh Shringla never missed being a playful boy who indulged in pranks and pillow fights. Despite being a naughty child, Harsh Shringla was a born leader. His leadership qualities and organising abilities were always on display. He was a good team leader who used to mobilise his cousins.

Neena remained close to her cousin even after his becoming Foreign Secretary. Those childhood bonds remained unfettered. Neena fondly recollects how Harsh Shringla continues to be deeply connected and affectionate. Whenever he visited them, he would make it a point to bring gifts according to the interests and tastes of each one of their family and friends. He remained a "loving and affectionate boy" who did not change with time and his positions. Beyond all these things, Neena highly admires how Harsh Shringla takes care of his parents, particularly his mother. Despite his busy schedule as Foreign Secretary, he made it a point to check whether his mother was having timely food and attends to her other requirements, personally.

He grew up immersed in the broader Indian-Nepali culture. He is simultaneously steeped in the traditional culture of his native area, its customs, its institutions, and its emphasis on respect for elders and for family.

The emphasis on education is confirmed by Suberna. Their father was sent by his father to the same primary school as his driver and other employees. Given his experience, he always felt his children should receive the best education. His father completed his Masters in Economics from the prestigious Calcutta University and secured a job in Government with the Forward Markets Commission. He later joined the Ministry of Commerce dealing with the import-export regulatory regime. Coming from the hills with no background whatsoever in Government service, this was considered a path-breaking initiative in his circles. His first posting was in Mumbai. Again, for someone without any exposure to a major city outside of Calcutta, setting up a de novo existence in a completely new large metropolitan environment would have been a challenging experience. Shringla's father was single at the time. He was married in Bombay later. While several relatives went on to study abroad at top institutions like Harvard and Stanford, Shringla's father was more focused on working in India, and went on to hold senior economic assignments.

T. T. La, was affable, humorous, and friendly towards all. He did not let the petty politics of office or family get the better of him. Beyond his outgoing and socially positive demeanour, T. T. La was a highly ambitious individual who wanted only the best for his family. He had a burning desire for his children to succeed where he felt he had not. In fact, a good part of Shringla's success can be attributed to his father's influence and drive, and his mother's focused energy and commitment to see their sons succeed.

Harsh Shringla's mother had a strong influence on him. She is of Nepali and Hindu ethnicity and belonged to the Basnet clan from the Jalapahar locality of Darjeeling. According to cousin Neena, she was one of the most beautiful women during her time in Darjeeling and remains extremely gracious and beautiful. Hari Devi was from a proud Nepalese family. Her father had, early on, joined the British Army and was deployed in Burma with his family. When he passed away suddenly at an early age, her mother, Dil Maya Basnet, was in a predicament to support 10 children without any means of income, and struggled to make ends meet. It was her eldest son, who joined the army at an early age and brought home a minimal income, that enabled the family to survive those difficult pre-World War II days. With the Japanese making a lightning offensive into Burma, the Basnet family was lucky to catch the last boat out of Burma into India. Thence started a new life and a new beginning for the Basnet family.

Harsh Shringla's mother speaks of the difficulty days when her mother had shifted to Darjeeling with her children with hardly any savings to fall back on. They settled down in Chundura village in Jalapahar where they found employment stitching uniforms and clothes for the Army Cantonment at Jalapahar. Mrs. Hari Devi recalls that in those difficult times how the Church approached her mother offering to take care of the family's schooling and wellbeing if she converted to Christianity, his grandmother, Dil Maya flatly refused, saying she would rather face starvation than compromise on her spirituality.

Many years later, when he was High Commissioner to Bangladesh, Harsh Shringla took his mother back to the Cantonment and the path to Chundura village—a walk down memory lane. Shringla remembers the carefree times he and his brother had spent there as children, being exposed directly to farming, nature and playing with the children of the village. Interestingly, at his UPSC interview, when Shringla was asked whether he had any exposure to a village he referred to his time in Chundura—

although the panellists were somewhat doubtful whether this village at the edges of a town could be compared to the rural village of their conception.

The strong focus on education and service ran across the wider family circle. It is difficult for an Indian to join the elite Indian Foreign Service. Becoming a Foreign Secretary of India is a dream for every Indian Foreign Service officer but only a few can achieve this distinction. It is rare for an Indian Foreign Service officer to rise to become Foreign Secretary and head the IFS. Several families have more than one family member in the service. Only two families in India have, however, produced more than one Foreign Secretary, one of them is the legendary Menons and the other, Shringla's extended family. His aunt, Chokila Iyer was India's first female Foreign Secretary between March 2001 to June 2002. Chokila Iyer's entry into the IFS had a great impact on him and by the time he was in high school, he knew that he wanted to join the IFS.

One of the lesser-known members of that family is Deputy Superintendent of Police Sonam Wangdi of the West Bengal Police. He was felled by a shower of arrows in Naxalbari in West Bengal in 1967. The ultra-leftist Naxal agitation—which was to later consume West Bengal, and remains active—had claimed Harsh Shringla's uncle as its first martyr. Shringla remains close to Inspector Wangdi's daughter and his cousin, Dechen Wangdi. She feels proud of the fact that 18 years later, Shringla occupied the same chair in the Ministry of External Affairs as his aunt had in 2001.

Harsh Shringla's composite identity did not emerge by accident. Darjeeling has an ethnic composition and culture that reflect its Himalayan location and trans-Himalayan Tibetan and Nepali influences. Hinduism and Buddhism coexist in harmony and spiritually sustain the people. His father's family were devout Buddhists but his father was a man who practised Hinduism as much as Buddhism and was a regular patron of both Buddhist monasteries and Hindu temples. His father regularly took him to the famous Kalibari temple in Calcutta, where the *pandas* knew his father, and darshan was swiftly arranged. His mother's family was very proud of their Hindu heritage. Thus, respect was inculcated for both Hindu and Buddhist traditions. His brother Suberna says they celebrate all the festivals like Dasain, Diwali and Losar with joy and that both these traditions are very dear to them.

"Home means Darjeeling" to the Shringlas, and the brothers remain strongly connected to Darjeeling. Although Shringla himself was born in Mumbai, and his brother in Chennai (then Madras), holidays while growing up were always in Darjeeling. The parents were proud of their Darjeeling ancestry and made sure that the children became familiar with the town, its people, and the area around them. Holidays meant playing with children in Chowk Bazar and visiting cousins and relatives on the Mall Road where horse riding was always adventurous and fun. There were excursions to the Botanical Gardens, hiking, and travelling in the local area and further afield to Sikkim in Jeeps. Darjeeling had relatives along with the family's traditional business in the heart of town.

The outdoors was a part of Shringla's upbringing. He liked hiking a lot and became a serious mountaineer who trained at the Nehru Institute of Mountaineering in Uttarkashi and was a member of his school's expedition to Everest Base in 1977. This love of hiking came in useful later (in 1996) in his career when he was Liaison Officer to a group of pilgrims on the arduous trek to Manasarovar under the Kailash Manasarovar Yatra scheme, and still later as Joint Secretary when he literally walked miles across paddy fields and marshy terrain to inspect enclaves and adverse possession in the land border between India and Bangladesh.

His parents' emphasis on a holistic upbringing and an integrated approach to education meant that excursions and travel were a part of life. They believed in exposing him to different influences and experiences and emphasised a problem-solving attitude. It also meant stress on languages. Although Shringla speaks in English to his brother—a legacy of their boarding school days—he is comfortable in Nepali and tries to use it often.

He is also an avid sportsman who loves hockey and squash. This emphasis on fitness remained with him as he rose in life. One of his first social media posts after he arrived in Washington to take over as Ambassador was about going for a run on a cold January morning.

Neena recalls meeting Shringla in Washington, D.C. when he became Ambassador of India to the United States in 2019. She says he was the same as what she remembered of him as a boy. He was serious—and not about appearances or fancy clothes, or the trappings of position. He remained humble, affectionate and equally caring in his general approach. It was a shock for Neena to realise that this cousin, unchanged since he was a boy, held such a high position. Even though he was Ambassador and an officer of the highest rank, "he was still the same". Harsha Shringla met his wife Hemal in Paris where she was a student. It was a love marriage and both families sanctified it. The daughter of doctors (both parents were doctors), Hemal was intellectually inclined and liberal in her beliefs. Their son, Ashoka, was born in Mumbai, as were both of his parents. Unlike Harsha Shringla, who spent much of his early days in one school, Ashoka studied in different locations from New York to Durban and from Bangkok to Dhaka. Named after Emperor Asoka, who was Hindu but propagated Buddhism and ruled over the largest-ever Indian empire, Ashoka was a highly intelligent and somewhat sensitive child. While his schooling in different locations allowed him great variety and exposure to different cultures, it also deprived him of lasting friendships and camaraderie arising out of common schooling experiences. His one period of stability was the four years he spent in Delhi's Sardar Patel Vidyalaya, where he developed enduring friendships.

Unlike his father, Ashoka's inclination was towards the sciences. He was comfortable with quantitative subjects like Mathematics and Physics but found it difficult to cope with the humanities as subjects during school. Passing out of the American International School in Dhaka, Ashoka secured admission to the prestigious New York University's School of

Engineering for Computer Science. Settling down for the first time, thousands of kilometres away from home was harder than either his parents or he imagined. His father's posting to the US a year later was an emotional game changer for Ashoka. By the time Harsh Shringla finished his term in the US and returned as Foreign Secretary to Delhi, Ashoka had spent almost three years of his undergraduate studies and had adjusted to his new environment and university routine. He spent a few months interning with a computer firm based in Virginia. His performance so impressed his supervisor that he offered him a job upon graduation. Ashoka graduated from NYU in 2020 and began working on developing software in an area of his interest. He chose to continue to live and work in Brooklyn, paying periodic visits to the company's head office in Virginia when required.

2

SCHOOL AND COLLEGE

SCHOOL: MAYO COLLEGE

IN NOVEMBER 2017, Harsh Shringla received a surprise. He was selected by his alma mater, Mayo College, Ajmer, which is one of India's most famous schools, for the Outstanding Alumni Award that year. The JTM Gibson Award for Excellence, named after a legendary Mayo Principal, "Jack" Gibson, is given annually since 2007, to alumni who have, "consistent with Jack Gibson's ideals, made a difference to society". The school invited him to receive the prize from the Chief Guest, then Chief of Naval Staff, Admiral S. Lanba, himself an alumnus.

A few years later, in November 2021, Shringla was invited to be the Chief Guest at the most important annual event held by the school, its prize-giving. He considered this to be "a full circle". In his inspiring address to the students, faculty, Governing Council, old boys, parents and others, who were attending the event dressed in their finest regalia, Shringla candidly spoke of the exceptional honour that the school had conferred on him. Addressing the students directly, he said that it seemed but a short time ago that he was sitting where they were, in full awe of the event and the dignitaries who were the year's Chief Guests. He was candid enough to say that he started off as a mediocre student in school but in keeping with his father's exhortations he never stopped trying his best. Over time, giving his best efforts to every endeavour that he was involved in, brought him back to school with the highest honours that his alma mater could bestow on him. Harsh Shringla had indeed come a full circle.

Joining him at the event were some of his closest friends, Altamush Kabir from Bangladesh, Somnath Jhala, Ghansham Singh, Rajiv Oberoi, Jagmohan, etc. Shringla also had the honour to present the Outstanding Alumni Award to two of his own classmates from school, Lt. Gen. Alok Kler (Retd.) and Air Marshal Rajesh Kumar (Retd.). It was a grand event with the colour and pageantry that the occasion demanded. He was excited to meet his Principal, Lt Gen (Retd.) Kulkarni, himself an old boy, a member of the school's Governing Council and his old teachers (S. M. Mathur, Ramesh Mathur, and Rozario), who were emotionally filled with his old memories that went back four decades. He was invited to inaugurate the new Alumni Office and Students' Counselling Centre. The event was conducted by Alumni Association President Col Bhawani Singh (Retd.), former Commanding Officer of the famous President's Bodyguard. Ajai Sirohi, Ajay Sachdeva and other members of the Mayo Alumni hockey team that visited him in Bangkok when he was Ambassador there also used the occasion to felicitate Shringla for his support to his school and its alumni.

Mayo College (school), which Harsh Shringla joined in 1971, at the age of 9, was set up in 1875 in Ajmer, Rajasthan. It was one of the first schools of its type, a boarding school, set up on the lines of fabled English public schools such as Eton College. The first students were the scions of Indian princely states. The school attempted to turn them into an upright and capable ruling class using the principles of modern education, as they were then understood. Mayo changed with the times but it is a testament to its DNA that it consistently ranks—more than a century after it was founded—among the best schools in India to date. Mayo is a residential all-boys school. It adopted the English public-school system of "Houses" which gives the boys a primary point of reference. Boarding schools such as Mayo believe in what is now often called a "holistic" approach to education. Academic rigour is accompanied by an emphasis on building character and resilience through physical, and outdoor activities, and extra-curricular activities. Students were literally expected to try everything. These included a variety of sports, theatre, trekking, the NCC, arts and crafts. The objective is to produce well-rounded individuals.

Harsh Shringla's brother, Suberna followed him to Mayo—also at the age of 9. It is interesting to note that Shringla's parents, in the early 1970s, chose not to send him to boarding schools in Darjeeling such as St. Paul's. India had barely been independent for two decades and the national identity was still evolving. The decision by his parents to entrust the schooling of their sons to a school located in the deserts of Rajasthan, far from home, says something about his parents' commitment to national integration and their focus on making their children independent, while simultaneously broadening their horizons. This certainly was not the norm at that time. It was very much an exception. North-East India was something of a mystery and it was unusual to see people from that region in Delhi and in other parts of India. Shringla and his brother stood out in school and outside—though things have changed substantially since then as people from North-Eastern states are much more visible in the national mainstream. This, however, makes Shringla something of a pioneer.

Mayo obviously was good for the Shringla brothers. Suberna recalls that boarding school had its challenges but it was ultimately a good life that the brothers enjoyed. When Shringla joined the school, he was given what is referred to as a double promotion: he was advanced for his age and the school found, while examining him, that he could actually jump two grades. Mayo was the kind of school that recognised this ability and moved him up. This jump created difficulties for Shringla in adjusting to the academic curriculum for the first few years in school but it later helped him when he graduated from university at a relatively young age. This, in turn, allowed him to join the IFS at the age of 22—one of the youngest to do so—and acquire an unusual depth of professional experience and variety.

Harsh Shringla spent his formative years in the school. It was clear that he was unusually mature for his age—almost precocious. He stood out due to his seriousness and what his brother describes as his "toughness". He was also unusually focused and ambitious.

Boarding schoolboys know each other extremely well. They know each other's characters and strengths and weaknesses. He made many lifelong friends in school. One of his friends, Leo Puri, recalls both his thoughtful nature and his balance and maturity. He also pointed out that Mr. Shringla has a natural restraint and humility. He was a "quiet reassuring presence, a reliable friend, who was never judgmental. If one did not know him well, one might even underestimate him." He made the insightful observation that Shringla, though quiet, "is not an introvert, he is stoic". He participated vigorously in all activities. This ability to combine activity with calmness contributed to his later success as a distinguished diplomat and policymaker.

Harsh Shringla read and continues to read a lot. Even during his schooldays, he delved into philosophy, history and foreign affairs. Somewhat unusual for a boy of his age and station, he memorised famous speeches and recorded himself declaiming them in front of a mirror. Suberna remembers him playing back speeches of Napoleon and Caesar repeatedly to master them. He was a perfectionist even then, as he is now.

It must be recalled that he went about systematically acquiring knowledge and building himself when there was no internet and no mobile phone, no YouTube and no Google.

Shringla was a hero to his brother who was in senior school when Suberna joined the preparatory school. He recalls a brother who was not just protective but an inspiration. A brother who appeared destined for bigger things. He was also not just capable, but ambitious. It was almost as if he already had a destination in mind and was working his way towards it from his schooldays. Many of his contemporaries shared the impression that he was fated to be someone important. In the words of one of his contemporaries, he was not "the usual kid". He was too purposeful and too serious for that.

Under the protective umbrella of his brother, Suberna excelled in school. He attained the highest and most prestigious position among students, that of School Captain, a post he held at a time when Mayo commemorated its 100th anniversary. Suberna recalls when in his capacity as School Captain he was required to receive the Chief Guest at Prize Giving at this occasion, the Sultan of Oman, who presented him with a gold watch as a mark of appreciation. Suberna was a natural all-rounder, winning awards for dramatics and debating and captaining the school in hockey, football, athletics and boxing. Like his brother, he too joined St. Stephen's College and then opted for a successful career in management after completing his Masters in Business Administration in Paris, France.

The period in school—combined with their father's transferable job—turned the Shringla brothers into cosmopolitan Indians, but they made every effort to introduced their friends to their part of world, their roots to Darjeeling Himalayas. Leo Puri recalls an exciting school trip to Everest Base camp and discovering that Shringla was a natural trekker. He also discovered his deep and distinguished family ties with the region. These were invaluable when they had to plan the trip or deal with the emergencies that arose. Meeting his family and relatives provided insight into their values, their standing, and their tradition of service. Mayo school environment, with its students from fascinating and diverse backgrounds, drew students into the national fabric organically as no lectures on unity in diversity were needed to integrate students from diverse background.

Shringla remains loyal to his school and friends. Many of them remained in touch with him and followed him as he ascended through the ranks of the Indian Foreign Service. His attachment to his school was obvious when, years later, as ambassador to Thailand, he organised the participation of a Mayo team in a regional hockey tournament.

ST. STEPHEN'S COLLEGE

In the summer of 1979, Harsh Shringla found himself doing the rounds of colleges at Delhi University. The competition was intense and there was no guarantee of securing entry into the best colleges. He applied to some of the top colleges, including St. Stephen's, Hindu, and Shri Ram College of Commerce. However, he was keen on securing a seat in an Honours course in the humanities. His marks in the CBSE exams got him beyond the cut-off and secured him an interview for History Honours at St. Stephen's College. He was interviewed by the formidable Padma Bhushan awardee, Prof. Mohammad Amin and was gratified to find his name in the final list of admissions to the college.

St. Stephen's College is acknowledged to be amongst the finest colleges in India. It is very selective in whom it admits. Its student body is of an incredibly high academic calibre. To this day, the humanities or "Arts" courses, such as History, which Shringla joined, have the highest "cut-offs" for admission. The academic strength of the students and the atmosphere of the college made it a nursery for future leaders. For Shringla, this was in some ways a natural movement because he had moved from one of the best schools in India to one of its best colleges. He was obviously a student of exceptional potential.

After the restrictions of a boarding school, Harsh Shringla and his friends, who were all from boarding school backgrounds, revelled in the newfound freedoms of the university environment. Shringla focused on extra-curriculars and sports, played hockey for the college and was proud to sport the St. Stephen's College tracksuit. The routine was gruelling though. Every morning, he and his teammates jogged the 3-4 km from college over the ridge to Mori Gate where the college playing fields were located and after a brisk warm-up, they had an intense hour of hockey practice. Thereafter, it was a jog back to college where a nimbu paani was waiting for them at Rohtas dhaba, courtesy of the college sports budget.

Shringla also actively participated in other college extra-curriculars and soon built up a network of friends and close associates. In the first year itself, and to his pleasant surprise, he was elected to the college council. As a college resident, he also came across students from different parts of the country. As someone who had lived in cities like Mumbai, Chennai, Kolkata, Ahmedabad, and Bangalore, he had a unique pan-India perspective. However, making friends with fellow students from different parts of India reinforced his sentiment about the uniqueness of the country in terms of both its diversity and inclusivity. He has continued to keep in touch with his circle of friends, many of whom interacted with him from time to time.

Through his formative years in school and college, some traits in Shringla's character were already obvious. A student who worked his way through Mayo, with a double promotion, and through St. Stephen's on merit was evidently an intelligent and hard-working young man. Along the way, he developed a loyal band of friends, with whom he continues to remain in touch. There is a consistency in the manner in which they speak of the young Harsh Shringla. The traits that come out most strongly are his integrity, his staunch loyalty, and his kindness. Even during his school

Parents Smt Hari Devi and father Late Shri TT LA

Harsh Shringla, Hemal Shringla, Ashok Vardhan Shringla, Suberna Shringla, Late Shri TT LA, Smt Hari Devi

Friendships that are Enduring: At St. Stephen's College In 1979

With Friends at the Lal Bahadur Shastri National Academy of Administration, Mussoorie in 1984

At Capetown, South Africa in 2009

and college days, he went out of his way to help people. One of his friends describes him as a "Shahenshah of friendship". This was a characteristic that stayed with him throughout his career and in life. He is able to attract enormous loyalty among his colleagues. He is a true team player.

He was also a very patient person who was always composed and "never lost his cool". His courtesy and his manners remain impeccable. His humility, and his down-to-earth character, were also obvious. These were traits that were evident in later years as he handled some of the toughest jobs in his field of work with a calm and steady approach. Shringla did not change as he rose in life. He was a voracious reader who was organised and meticulous in his habits. He had a gift for languages. In the course of his career, he would learn to do business in Vietnamese, French, Bangla and Nepalese.

Boarding school and college instilled not only grit and humility but also a sense of fairness and fair play. He always was—and remains—willing to listen to other points of view. Through all of this, the picture that emerges is of a highly-motivated, sincere and driven young man; a person who wanted to do big things; and do it the right way. These qualities that were inculcated in the boarding schools formed a hallmark of his personality and career.

On its part, St Stephen's College also acknowledged his contribution by conferring on him an extraordinary recognition, the 'Order of Illustrious Stephanians', along with a few other luminaries, including his illustrious senior colleague, Shiv Shankar Menon. At his acceptance address, Shringla encouraged young students to devote their careers to public service and offered to mentor young Stephanians who decided to take this path.

3

EARLY EMPLOYMENT AND CIVIL SERVICE EXAMINATION

EARLY EMPLOYMENT

HARSH SHRINGLA graduated at the relatively young age of 19. St. Stephen's was one of India's prestigious colleges and a recruiting ground for some of India's best corporate houses. In the days before liberalisation and before engineering and business schools had acquired their current stature, St. Stephen's was one of the few institutions in India which had campus placements.

He was barely out of college when he had two good job offers in hand. It was always his belief that one should remain as productive as possible. This naturally led to the need to join the workforce as early as possible. While most opted for postgraduate studies, he looked at building valuable work experience. In his final year at college, a number of campus interviews were conducted and he selectively participated in a few.

A campus interview that attracted his attention early was from a top-ranked tea broking firm called J. Thomas & Co. Pvt. Ltd. After a series of written tests, interviews and group discussions, he sufficiently impressed the interviewers and was called for a final round of interviews in Calcutta. Selected with him were a few of his closest friends from college. They travelled together and made a great outing. However, in the group discussion, Shringla excelled. Later, J Thomas informed him that he was the only one from the entire campus interview process who had been selected.

J. Thomas & Co. Pvt. Ltd was a highly-rated firm with a good record of profitability. The company traditionally recruited very few people but had a reputation for looking after its own. Those who made the grade were extensively trained in India and abroad. Shringla was pleased with his very first job offer and was keen to join the firm. However, he was soon to receive other job offers of interest that were in line with his preference for a career in management. He did regret that giving up J. Thomas & Co. Pvt. Ltd offer did not mean this would go to one of his friends who were with him in the final round of interviews.

An exciting new opportunity came in the form of campus interviews conducted by a leading multinational, Brooke Bond India Limited. The company had earlier recruited some of Shringla's close friends. This opened up a whole new exciting prospect. Brooke Bond's selection process was even more difficult than that of J. Thomas & Co. Pvt. Ltd. There were many more candidates shortlisted from some of the best colleges in Delhi. The interview process was gruelling and it was the group discussion that decided the winners from the losers. He was struck by how some of his classmates, who were so highly rated as star sportsmen and leading icons, failed to utter a single word during the group discussions.

On his part, Shringla adopted a clever tactic for the group discussions. He had been well coached by some of his friends who had successfully gone through the process. Normally, the format called for the participants themselves to decide on a topic of their choice for discussion. The trick was not to speak at the very beginning but to allow others to voice their views. Intervening was best if it came at a critical stage that allowed a summary of the various views and the presentation of a convincing argument that would seal the choice of topic. Shringla argued in favour of the topic of energy security and the importance of India's relations with the Gulf countries in this regard. Since it was the days of increasing fuel prices and oil embargoes, this was a topical and timely subject for discussion. Tactically, he supported the weaker participants against the more self-assured ones. Again, the idea was not to wade into the discussion but to make occasional interventions that summarised the existing threads of the discussions and to lead the conversation in a logical manner.

Shringla was selected for the final round in Bangalore, where he successfully used the same tactics in the group discussion. His moment of satisfaction came when he was seated with all the other candidates and the receptionist called out his name and asked him to enter the office. There he found the Chairman and the entire Board of Brooke Bond present. They watched every step of the interview and group discussion process. As in the case of J. Thomas & Co. Pvt. Ltd, here, again, the Chairman informed him that he was the only candidate selected. He never saw the other candidates again. He felt sorry for some of his close friends who had made it to the final round with him but could not bag the job.

Barely 20 and out of college, Shringla embarked on a new phase in his life. While others opted for postgraduate degrees, he had always believed that the best knowledge came with practical on-the-job experience. And Brooke Bond India provided the ideal learning ground. He started at corporate headquarters in Bangalore and thereafter went through a year's training at Coimbatore, Delhi, Chandigarh and Calcutta before being posted on his first assignment as a Management Trainee in Sales to Akola in Maharashtra.

Akola was a remote mofussil town in the cotton belt of western Maharashtra. It was the ideal training ground for someone selling tea. Paradoxically, even though Akola was one of the hottest spots in India, it consumed large quantities of tea. Hence it was a great market for Brooke Bond India's packaged teas, with demand often exceeding supply. However, for a 21-year-old, Akola was not the place of dreams though it reminded him of his home, Darjeeling which produces world-class tea; nevertheless, he did stay in a place called Dreamland Lodge. Shringla decided to quit and devote himself full-time to preparing for the Civil Services exam. This was the ultimate dream he had harboured since childhood.

This is the one inflection point in his life where he actually quit. Although his decision was vindicated by the success of his efforts later, Shringla always saw the decision in Akola as an act of weakness. His maxim of "a winner never quits and a quitter never wins" was reinforced by the experience in Akola and stayed with him for the rest of his life. Thus, began a new page in his life and career.

THE CIVIL SERVICE EXAMINATION

With no job in hand, Harsh Shringla knew he had few options but to succeed in his endeavour to join the higher civil service. He had always been inspired by his father, a civil servant, and had aspired to join the Indian Foreign Service. Although he had been diverted to a career in management due to his experience of working in Brooke Bond India, his unwavering ambition to become India's diplomat compelled him to quit this job. He was now back to his original goal of aspiring to a place in the civil service.

Upon resigning from Brooke Bond, he had just enough time to appear for the preliminary test of the civil services examination, or the "prelims". Fortunately, he had, even while he was in Brooke Bond, filled in and submitted his application form for the civil services exam. This measure of abundant precaution held him in good stead. Within a few days of his resignation from Brooke Bond, he was headed for Calcutta, which he had listed as his centre for the exam. He had chosen history as optional and general studies as mandatory. In Calcutta, he linked up with his college mate and neighbour in the hostel, Bani Brata Bhattacharya, who was another aspirant for the civil services. Being great friends they both went together to the same centre for their prelims. Bani Bhattacharya was great company, a fun-loving individual. He was selected for the Customs Service where he had an illustrious career as one of the most upright and effective customs officers. He was known as the scourge of Bombay's main market for illicit goods. Shringla also called on his uncle, Nima Tenduf, the eternal Captain of the Indian Army. Captain Uncle, as he was affectionately known, was unfortunately very unwell and in a coma at the Command Hospital in Calcutta. It was his last visit to Captain Uncle, who passed away a few months later. He was also able to link up with his good friend and college mate, Philip Mani, who later quit Brooke Bond India to study in Cambridge and subsequently joined the British Foreign Service.

A few months later, on a rainy monsoon evening, Harsh Shringla went, along with Philip Mani, to the famous UPSC building on Shahjahan Road in New Delhi to check his preliminary exam results. In those days, the results were posted on the UPSC notice board and candidates had to go there to check whether they had succeeded. Philip Mani had accompanied him and he was relieved to find his name on the list confirming that he had made it through the challenging first stage of the exam.

Harsh Shringla started a gruelling schedule of preparation for the second and main civil service examination or "Mains". While his subject at university was History, he needed to identify one more optional for the Mains. He settled on Sociology, a subject he felt would be both interesting and easier to master. He did realise, however, that intense studies by themselves would not be enough to give him an edge in a highly competitive process for which he would have less than six months of preparation. He opted, therefore, for coaching at the famous Rau's IAS Study Circle.

Mr. Rau, who personally ran the centre, was an interesting and accomplished personality. It was rumoured that having failed to clear the competitive exam, Mr. Rau had spent his life preparing others to succeed where he did not. Shringla got to know Mr. Rau very well over the next few months and began to look up to him. He was highly disciplined and principled, full of anecdotes of life and living. What was important, however, was that Mr. Rau provided his students with the best inputs that could give them that vital edge over others in a highly competitive process. In the first place, Mr. Rau only selected candidates who, he felt, stood a good chance at mastering the exams and then went on to intensively coach the selected few in their subjects.

Shringla opted for special coaching in Sociology and General Studies for the mains, and later, for the personality test, or the "interview". Mr. Rau provided specialised notes on all important areas of preparation for the optional papers. Classes were conducted for half a day after which students were required to prepare at home. What actually made the difference were the specialised techniques for writing the exams that Rau provided his students. For instance, Mr. Rau constantly emphasised the need for all answers to be strictly confined to the prescribed word limit. If the word limit for an answer was 500, it was essential that one counted the words and made sure that the answer did not exceed that limit. This was very valuable for History students such as Shringla, who had always functioned in an environment where the lengthier the answer, the better the likely result. The UPSC process was clearly designed to test the academic discipline of the candidates as much as their substantive knowledge.

Shringla enjoyed the intense academic environment at Rau's and applied himself to the task at hand assiduously. He spent every waking hour on his books and his notes. It was six months of exclusive preparation for the UPSC exam without any diversion of attention. Fortunately, his parents had a flat in Delhi and his mother stayed there to ensure that not only were his food and other requirements looked after but that he was not disturbed at all.

When the day of the exams finally arrived, Shringla felt he was fully prepared. He had learned by rote every single word in the *India Digest* and the general studies curriculum. The exams themselves involved writing eight papers (4 optional, 2 General Studies, 1 English and 1 Hindi qualifying paper) for three hours each. It was a gruelling process that required appearing for eight papers over 3-4 days. Many candidates actually suffered intense anxiety or nervous breakdowns when the actual time came. One of his friends from college, who was a brilliant student, actually collapsed from sheer fatigue, and possibly anxiety, while appearing for one of the papers, and had to be evacuated from the UPSC building. Shringla, however, was confident, and even cautiously optimistic. Many of his friends had parents who met them with tiffin in the lunch break between exams. Shringla did not need such pampering, and in fact used the break between the papers to revise and greet friends, many of whom were also appearing for the exams at the same time.

Shringla found that six months of preparation had given him sufficient confidence to handle the written examination. He felt he had done well in some papers, while he had some doubts about how he would be evaluated in others. At least one each of his History and Sociology papers had questions that were conceptual in nature. While he developed a line of thought in responding to these questions, he could not be sure if the examiner would agree with his perspective. It would have been easier to predict the outcome of questions that called for factual answers. For example, one of the General Studies papers was based on factual parameters, such as sections of the Indian Constitution, etc. It was possible to get a fair sense of whether one was right or wrong on these questions. As it happened, Shringla received his highest marks in the papers that involved an examination of the candidate's thinking and analytical abilities more than a regurgitation of facts.

In November 1983, Harsh Shringla once again made the trip to the UPSC building. To his relief, he found that he had cleared the Mains and was cleared to prepare for the last phase of the civil service exam process, the interview. He had some time to prepare for his interviews. Here again, Mr. Rau provided useful inputs, although he felt he was adequately prepared for the interview and less reliant on coaching than he was for the written examination. Having been to a range of job interviews, he felt that he had enough experience to deal with the UPSC interview.

Mr. Rau had also given him a sense of the disposition of the interview panels and their focus. There were a number of interview panels, each headed by a member of the UPSC. Shringla was fortunate in that his interview was conducted by an outstanding and highly supportive panel. The Chair was a kindly gentleman who steered the conversation in a convivial manner designed to put the candidate at ease. The panel included a former IAS and IFS officer. The latter was Ambassador Gurbachan Singh, who took special interest when he learned that his first choice was the IFS. The panel's questioning was eclectic in the true spirit of a process designed to select those with the best all-round abilities for general administrative functions. He remembered being asked for a description of the Holy Trinity. Shringla's response was to say the Holy Trinity he knew consisted of Brahma, Shiva and Vishnu. The panel reminded him that they had in mind the Christian Holy Trinity consisting of the Father, the Son and the Holy Ghost. They were gracious enough, however, to readily acknowledge that his response was equally correct.

The panel also asked him about OPEC, Brunei and the geographic location of Venezuela. One of the questions Shringla thoroughly enjoyed was on India's development programmes, which he had learned and memorised in great detail. He went on to describe various programmes and when he spoke of TRYSEM, the panel immediately stopped him and asked him to state its full form and description. He was happy to oblige. The panel also spent time on his exposure to rural India and he was ready with his experience of Akola in Maharashtra, his first assignment as a Management Trainee at Brooke Bond India, or in rural Darjeeling where his aunt lived.

All in all, Shringla felt he had acquitted himself well in the interview process and expected the interview results to bolster his overall ranking. When the results came, he found that he had received 215 out of 250 (86%) in the interview process. Undoubtedly, there were some who did better but, in general, the interview results definitely improved his overall ranking in a highly competitive process.

WAITING FOR THE RESULTS

Immediately after his interview, Shringla proceeded to Gangtok, Sikkim, where the wedding of his favourite cousin, Sharab Shringla (Lulu), was being held. Lulu was the son of his aunt on his father's side, and very close to his father. Having lost both his parents at an early age, Lulu was a self-made man. Intelligent and sensitive, Lulu was one of his role models and mentors. Having completed his schooling and graduated from the famous St. Joseph's College in Darjeeling, Lulu got admission to the prestigious XLRI Institute of Management in Jamshedpur. Shringla recalls spending a memorable few weeks with Lulu in Kuwait where he was the Manager of the State Trading Corporation of India.

Shringla recalls travelling from Bagdogra airport to Gangtok, he shared a taxi with two ladies, who were prominent in business and professional life in Sikkim. The conversation centred around the UPSC exams that he had just appeared for; while still in his examination mode he expressed strong determination to crack the process. He was emphatic in stating that if he did not succeed, he would persevere until he succeeded. The ladies were impressed by the young man's sense of determination.

Shringla found Sikkim to be a clean and relatively well-managed state. The wedding was celebrated in a hotel with great enthusiasm. Besides the usual traditional dances, there were generous amounts of the local millet beer called 'Chang', going around. On his return to Delhi, while awaiting the outcome of the exam, Shringla applied for management vacancies in Air India and also appeared for the entrance examination for the Indian Institute of Management.

CIVIL SERVICE EXAM RESULTS

When the civil service exam results were finally announced in April 1984, Shringla found that he had done well enough to attain his dream of being recruited to the Indian Foreign Service. He passed the exam when he was 22 years old, making him one of the youngest officers to join this elite service.

It was August 1984 and Shringla had already settled down in his new job at Air India headquarters in Mumbai when the UPSC's final results were due. Given the ratio of 1 out of every 2 persons called for the interview making it to some service, Shringla was reasonably certain that he would figure in the merit list. The question was where exactly he would figure. If he was below a certain position in the merit list, he would be eligible for less sought-after services. He would have to decide between retaining his job as an executive officer in the Planning and International Relations Department of Air India or joining the service. What made it more difficult for Shringla was a letter he received just then confirming his admission into the MBA programme of the Indian Institute of Management, Calcutta. Shringla had stood for the IIM exams after the UPSC exam and had been called for an interview. At his interview in Delhi, he was surprised when his interviewers declared him successful after only a few short questions. On his inquiry, the chair of the interview board informed him that as the only non-IIT interviewee and the only one with any job experience, Shringla was a natural candidate for the prestigious MBA programme.

The results took some time to be announced and there was some anxiety in the Shringla family. Every day brought the promise of results being declared only to face disappointment. On the actual day of the results, Shringla did a long commute from his office in Nariman Point to his flat at Juhu. While strolling down the last few metres to his building, Shringla saw his brother waving to him from above in an excited manner. Later, his brother Suberna told him that he had been trying to signal to him the number fifteen. Shringla had successfully qualified for the Civil Services exam and stood 15th in the All-India Civil Services list, which meant he had qualified for the much sought-after Indian Foreign Service. Harsh Shringla's determination and hard work paid off, and then began the saga of his illustrious career.

Shringla overnight received accolades and felicitations from far and wide. *Competition Success Review*, the leading brand magazine for the Civil Services Exam, immediately sought an interview. A number of universities and institutes requested his guidance for Civil Service aspirants. His stock rose even among his extended family members, some of whom were unabashed in their transformation from indifference to adulation. In Air India, from being the lowest-ranking officer, Shringla became a minor celebrity. His Executive Director, Shri S. K. Datta hosted a felicitation dinner for the entire Department in honour of his success. What was ironic was that it was virtually impossible in the normal course to even get a glimpse of S. K. Datta, who was the omnipotent head of the department. Nevertheless, Shringla maintained close contact with S. K. Datta, who, like almost all of his known colleagues and associates in Air India, left and joined the more lucrative Gulf carriers. Shringla also continued his contact with his friends Shankar Chatterjee, Suresh Lakshman, Bhagwat, Gupte, Sadanandam and other friends from his Air India days.

Mr. Suresh Lakshman recalls 21-year-old Shringla joining Air India as ASS (Assistant Station Superintendent) "He was one of the most introverted in terms of shyness but a very talented person." The moment Lakshman met him he noticed "a spark in his eye" and knew that "this guy had come to learn and go on further". He asserts that Shringla catches things very fast, "he catches it immediately when someone tells him something and delivers it with satisfaction".

With that spark and enthusiasm, Lakshman was not surprised when Shringla got into foreign service directly. Apart from the shyness at that point in time, Lakshman states that once "he knows people, he is always friendly and out there to help and reach. He was gentlemanly in manners, well-behaved and he would take orders very politely. He put his opinion in a way that everybody opens up. He had a broad mind." That is where diplomacy came, which Lakshman didn't realise at that point in time.

4

JOINING THE INDIAN FOREIGN SERVICE

INITIATION INTO SERVICE

HARSH SHRINGLA had always aspired to join the Indian Foreign Service. It had been his dream and that of his father and finally years of hard work and preparation had paid off.

The civil service, particularly the higher civil service, is considered to be an elite within India. The nature of the job, the senior positions occupied by civil servants, and the opportunity of working for the public good made it the most sought-after profession in the country. The Indian Foreign Service was, and remains, an elite within this elite. Like all elites, it is relatively small in numbers, highly trained and meritocratic in culture. Its job—that of representing India across the world, and working on the substance and form of international relations—is endlessly fascinating.

In 1984 when Harsh Shringla joined the IFS, he was one of the few officers from Darjeeling and Sikkim. His aunt, Chokila Iyer, Rinzing Wangdi, and Tsewang Topden preceded him and very few succeeded him. A 22-year-old Shringla was joining a service that was only 36 years old. He belonged, in a sense, to the first generation born after independence and he joined the service when India "was very different from what it is today". As of today, India is a major power and is on the trajectory to great power status. The year 1984 was a difficult year. It was the year the Government moved decisively to battle terrorism in Punjab. Prime Minister Indira Gandhi was assassinated a few months thereafter. This was also the pre-economic reform India associated with the desultory so-called "Hindu rate of growth". The years of India as an emerging economy were still decades into the future.

Joining in 1984 placed Shringla in the 1984 "batch". The Indian Foreign Service, which was descended from the Indian Political Service, which recruited the brightest officers of the colonial Indian Army and the legendary Indian Civil Service, had started developing its own traditions and rituals. The "batch" trained together and stayed together. The training was based on a combination of academy-based curricula and on-the-job training supervised by a mentor. The Indian Foreign Service, because of the nature of its responsibilities abroad, imparted additional elements of training such as the requirement of compulsorily learning a foreign language.

His batch consisted of some brilliant individuals. In the idiom of the service, Shringla ranked third in seniority in his batch after Dr. Atul Khare and Uma Ratnam. Dr. Khare, an AIIMS doctor, moved to the United Nations after an illustrious career and today is the seniormost international civil servant in the UN Secretariat. Uma left the service to join the private sector. Anup Mudgal, later High Commissioner in Mauritius; Mukta Dutta

Tomar, who retired as Ambassador in Germany; Gautam Bambawale, one of India's most respected experts in China and Ambassador to Beijing; Debnath Shaw, Rajesh Sachdeva, Sanjiv Arora, Nandini Krishna Iyer and Krishan Kumar were his other batchmates.

The bond within the batch is considered by civil servants to be amongst the most special. The first day in the service and how the batchmates meet for the first time become a part of the special folklore that is unique to each such batch. The first introduction of Indian Foreign Service officers to the Ministry of External Affairs is when they walk in to join it in the South Block. To many this majestic building which the Ministry shares with the Prime Minister's Office and with the Ministry of Defence is hallowed ground.

In August 1984, when Shringla entered South Block from Gate 5, which is now the Prime Minister's Office, he remembers seeing "a very confident young lady in a yellow sari also entering the office from Gate 5". This turned out to be Mukta Dutta (Tomar), one of Shringla's close friends who retired as Ambassador of India to Germany. Shringla remembers the first week of orientation with the only Foreign Service Officer that would be known to him until a later part of the training, Ambassador Vivek Katju, who was then Under Secretary (Foreign Service Personnel) and later went on to become Secretary (West) in the Ministry.

The first phase of training for officers is conducted at the Lal Bahadur Shastri National Academy of Administration (LBSNAA) in Mussoorie in the Himalayas. This legendary establishment, home of the Indian Administrative Service, also conducts what is called the Foundation Course for fresh entrants to IFS along with IAS.

Shringla fitted in easily at the Lal Bahadur Shastri National Academy of Administration. The sprawling campus and emphasis on extra-curricular activity were reminiscent of school for him. Probationers, as they were called, came from all over the country to join different services, from the elite IAS to the Allied Services. The different activities from cross-country to excursions encouraged the development of a strong esprit de corps, something that was to prove useful as careers progressed. Shringla made good friendships, some of which remained with him throughout his career.

As an avid hockey player, Shringla participated regularly in the practice sessions. It was an enjoyable experience for him. More importantly, it allowed the players to develop a good understanding of the field and emerge as a well-knit and coordinated team. As a hockey player, Shringla saw important lessons in life such as the need to focus and concentrate. He was inspired by the Mahabharata in which Arjun is advised by Krishna to keep his focus on the eye of the fish in the archery competition. Literally, "keep your eye on the ball", a dictum that he followed, not only on the hockey field but also in his personal and professional life.

Playing in a forward position, Shringla's task in the team was to move forward with the ball with the objective of scoring a goal. His experience in hockey taught him to take a shot at the goal as soon as it was opportune to do so. He knew that hesitation could prove costly. He had seen many of his teammates fritter away chances by trying to manoeuvre into better positions when they could well have taken a chance at the goal. One of Shringla's close friends in college was a very talented player and the joke about him was that he was so talented that he would use his skills to dribble past the defenders and the goalkeeper, sometimes even dribbling past the goal post, but Shringla was very clear "if you had a shot at the goal, you take it".

Harsh Shringla recalls a match with arch-rival, the Forest Research Institute in Dehradun. While the Mussoorie Academy trained the IAS and IFS, the Dehradun Institute trained Forest Service officers. Fitness was an important criterion in being selected for the Forest Service. The Academy team was naturally worried. They were playing against physically fit players who had a much longer training stint to hone their skills as a team. The Academy bus took the players and a cheering squad to the sprawling and beautiful Forest Institute campus in the plains of Dehradun just below the Mussoorie hills. It was hot in the afternoon and the game began with robustness. The Forest Institute team pressed forward keeping the pressure constantly on the Academy half. Defenders on the Academy side had a hard time while the forwards were left underutilised. Shringla moved back to lend a helping hand to the defenders of his team and to access the ball and take it away from his half. Fortunately, there were no goals until half-time. However, in the second half, a long shot reached Shringla who was close to the line on the right of the field. He quickly took advantage of the play by moving forward at a fast pace. Passing the ball to another teammate, he positioned himself ahead of the surging forward line. As the forwards thundered past a Forest Institute defence line caught off-guard, his teammate passed him the ball. He received the ball just inside the D (the designated area near the goal from which an opposing player can score a goal). It was still a long shot with maximum distance away from the goal and several defenders moving quickly to cut him off. Here's where the judgement was required, should he take the shot or position himself for a better play? There comes a tide in the affairs of men and hesitation can prove costly.

But Shringla did not hesitate, as he trapped the ball at the top of the D, he took a step forward and with an unerring shot scored the first goal for the Academy. Of course, he needed to weigh the options before him before going in for the shot at the goal. He realised that with the defenders closing in on him and his teammates behind him, dribbling inside the D could prove futile. His best option was to go for it. Even if the goalkeeper were to stop the ball, it offered scope for another chance on the rebound.

Shringla himself was surprised at the success of his shot. He was not sure he could do it. The odds were against him proving successful. Yet, he took the chance and scored the goal. What if he had waited for a better play, manoeuvred himself into a better position, or attempted a pass to another teammate? These are moot points. He saw his opportunity and he took it. He has always been an ardent follower of the Bhagavad

Gita, often recounting Krishna's advice to a hesitant Arjuna on the eve of the Mahabharata. While both the performance of an action and the renunciation of action were great, of these, the performance of action was greater than its renunciation. The moral of the story is, "if you see a shot in life, take it, use that killer instinct to be decisive and not hesitate when the time comes".

The experience at the Lal Bahadur Shastri National Academy of Administration was memorable to him. A three-month foundation course provided the basic inputs required for initial entrance into Government service and provided opportunities for extensive extra-curricular. It was a base to make friends and build an esprit de corps. While today's foundation course has been made competitive with probationers encouraged to compete further in a bid to enhance their positions in the inter-seniority list, many feels that the old model whereby the foundation course focused on building the essentials in young officers and holding them to high standards of bureaucracy after an already gruelling competitive examination process was more appropriate. Memorable among the different activities at Mussoorie was the village visit, which took Shringla to Lalitpur district in UP and a wonderful trek to Dodital in the Garhwal Himalayas. Many of his friends at Mussoorie continue to be Shringla's principal interlocutors in Government and elsewhere.

After Mussoorie, Harsh Shringla got a train directly to Cuttack, Orissa for a period of district training. He felt somewhat isolated, being the only probationer lodged in the Circuit House in Cuttack. However, the then District Collector, Mr. Harmohan Patnaik took him under his wing and provided him with first-hand experience in administering one of the most important districts and organising elections to four Lok Sabha constituencies in 1984. Shringla remembers travelling with Mr. Harmohan Patnaik, who's highly promising career was ended when he passed away at a young age. Shringla remembers Collector Patnaik berating BDOs and Tehsildars for non-performance. In all, it was an unforgettable and highly essential part of the training programme for young officers.

LANGUAGE TRAINEE

As was customary, after a year's training in Delhi at different institutes dealing with public administration, mass media, defence, culture, etc., each probationer was assigned a compulsory foreign language, which would also determine the place of his first posting. Indian Foreign Service officers are expected to compulsorily learn a foreign language. They remain on probation till they demonstrate by passing an examination that they are proficient in it. The language they learn also determines their first posting. Due to his seniority on the list, Shringla was assigned French, and in January of 1986, he left on his first foreign assignment to Paris.

Paris was not as Shringla expected. The city was cold and consistently grey, he only remembers travelling to the office by metro in the mornings when it was still dark and returning home under equally sombre conditions in the evening. His batchmate, Atul Khare and two officers of the previous batch, Satish Mehta and Kuldeep Bharadwaj, were a great support, but in the initial period, there were few friends and he had to often visit his collegemates in the UK. One of these close friends was Philip Mani who was doing his postgraduation at Cambridge University. Philip later took British citizenship and joined the British Foreign Service. He also remembers meeting some interesting characters at Cambridge, including an American student who lived on Cherry Hinton Street and wanted to join the US Foreign Service.

Later, as his grasp of the French language grew, and his ability to decipher French customs and traditions became more acute, Shringla began a slow appreciation of the city. Caught between learning a new language and working at UNESCO under a highly competent but driven Ambassador Arundhati Ghose, he had little time to appreciate the sights and sounds of Paris. What he did remember, however, were his 4 a.m. duties to receive dignitaries when the Air France flight from Delhi came in. Bleary-eyed, Shringla took recourse to the strong but effective Cafe Noir at Paris airport to sufficiently awaken him before he welcomed the arriving dignitary. It was only during his second term of office as First Secretary in Paris that he understood France, its culture and civilisation sufficiently, albeit grudgingly. However, it was only many years later, in September 2020, when Shringla visited Paris as Foreign Secretary that he fully appreciated what Paris had to offer. He also discovered a very different relationship, one in which India and France found a great deal of convergence and mutually beneficial cooperation.

POSTING TO VIETNAM

After completion of language training and passing the Compulsory Foreign Language examination, Harsh Shringla was sent to his first substantive posting to Vietnam in February 1988. Vietnam was a part of French Indo-China for almost 200 years. He reached Vietnam barely a decade after Vietnam was unified after a fiercely contested conflict between the Americans and the North Vietnamese Government.

After completing his language training and passing the Compulsory Foreign Language examination, Shringla was sent on his first substantive posting to Hanoi, the capital of Vietnam, in January 1988. Vietnam was a part of French Indo-China for almost 200 years. He reached Vietnam barely a decade after Vietnam was unified after a fiercely contested conflict between the Americans and the North Vietnamese Govt. Friends from that period remember a diligent officer who could speak very good French but began by learning Vietnamese.

After replacing Mr. Vijay Gokhale, who he later again succeeded as Foreign Secretary, and whom he considered as one of the most brilliant officers in the IFS, Shringla settled down quickly in Hanoi under the tutelage of Ambassador Pushkar Johari. The Embassy was a close-knit team with officers and their families helping each other in what was considered a difficult and hardship posting. Shringla recalls the kindness of his senior colleagues, Mr DJ Bell, Mr. Attri, Mr Ram Gopal and Military Attaches Col Cander Narayan and Col Mohinder Gill. He also made some lifelong friends in Suraender Baboo and Ashok Sharma and Khangserpa Dorjee (who died young on a posting in Kampala). Ambassador Pushkar Johari finished his term and was succeeded by a young and charismatic Ambassador, Arun Patwardhan. However, tragedy was soon to befall the family and the embassy in Hanoi.

On 13th September 1988, the Air Vietnam plane carrying Indian Ambassador Arun Patwardhan and his family and 15 other Indian nationals crashed near Bangkok airport during a major storm. Shringla had been asked to proceed on temporary duty to Seoul to help the Embassy with the Olympic Games there, and Shringla and his brother were booked on that flight. Just the day prior to departure, Ambassador Patwardhan received a message confirming his son's admission to University in New York for which he was required to proceed immediately. Ambassador Patwardhan and his wife decided to accompany their son up to Bangkok. He called Shringla and asked him to consider leaving two days later given the fact that the Embassy was short staffed. Shringla agreed, and they spent the eve of the journey at a convivial dinner at the Patwardhan's trying a Mongolian Hotpot dish along with Mrs. Chandrika Narayan, wife of the Military Attache. Early next morning, the Embassy received a message informing about the unfortunate crash in which all passengers had perished.

After that, the post of Ambassador remained vacant for some time until Mr. JC Sharma took over as Ambassador. A former Army officer, Ambassador JC Sharma had a can do spirit and would work differently from his predecessors. Shringla got to know him well and they remained in touch until many years later when Ambassador JC, as he was fondly known, passed away.

After completing his two-year term in Hanoi, the capital of Vietnam, Shringla volunteered to go to Ho Chi Minh City to open the Indian Consulate General there. This was the erstwhile Saigon, the capital of colonial French China and of the defeated South Vietnamese government, the commercial capital of Vietnam.

Mr. Atul Kumar, a prominent expatriate businessman, who met Harsh Shringla in 1987, recalls that Ho Chi Minh City had only four Indians at that time and Mr. Shringla, who came in with a team of two, built up the Consulate General of India in Ho Chi Minh City from scratch. He was very impressed by the sharp young IFS officer with an "elephantine memory" who in his second posting became the first Consul General in Ho Chi Minh City. "We were a very small community in Ho Chi Minh City at that time. No example like this could be given in this foreign service, in the second posting you get a promotion and also you go down to Ho Chi Minh City, a commercial capital in Vietnam as the Consul General. That was a great achievement I would say". While still in his twenties, Shringla was given his first big responsibility.

That is how his career started with a very big achievement. He stayed in Ho Chi Minh City for two years after two years in Hanoi. Therefore, the total exposure in Vietnam was four years. He recalls Shringla taking classes at the university there in Ho Chi Minh City and, in no time, he could speak fluent Vietnamese and that was the reason he could interact with people. Mr. Kumar says that he has not seen anybody who is so proactive with people and connects so well with people which makes Shringla so amazing. He remembers an incident when in meetings with Vietnamese people, Shringla would always listen to what the Vietnamese were talking about without them knowing that he could understand and speak fluent Vietnamese. At times, he would take Mr. Kumar aside and explain what those people were talking about. Nevertheless, later the Vietnamese delegates realised that he was well-versed in the language and started communicating in Vietnamese.

Mr. Kumar describes him as "a born leader, team worker who believes in the philosophy of giver" but never saw Shringla lose his temper or be aggressive. He never denied help to anyone who approached him and extended his hand to reach out to people. Many may consider this as his weakness, but his inherent strength is so strong that he does not waste time losing his temper, focusing instead on what needs to be done to the best of his capabilities.

Vietnam was one of Harsh Shringla's most memorable tenures. It was a time of great geopolitical change in India, the assassination of Rajiv Gandhi, and globally, the collapse of the Soviet Union, with its attendant impact on Vietnam that depended on the USSR for political and economic support, Young and impressionable, Vietnam left its impact on Shringla's psyche. He made some very good local friends in Tuyet, who still works at the Indian Consulate in Ho Chi Minh City, Du and Vinh, Thanh, Ha and Loan, among many others. But it was a time to move on and Shringla found himself back at the familiar stretch of the Champs Elyssees.

BACK TO PARIS

Harsh Shringla completed his tenure in Ho Chi Minh City in December 1991 and returned to the Embassy of India in Paris. He joined as First Secretary (Commercial) and Head of Chancery. He first served under Ambassador C. V. Ranganathan and then under Ambassador Ranjit Sethi.

Shringla's second assignment in Paris, 1992-1995 coincided with India's decision to go in for a massive structural adjustment or economic liberalisation programme under PM Narasimha Rao and Finance Minister Manmohan Singh. This period saw the country go from being a country dependent on foreign assistance to holding a surplus foreign exchange balance. Shringla recalls how the annual meeting of the Aid India Consortium, which brought together donor countries and organisations, was the most important event in the diplomatic calendar. He recalls observing stalwarts like Montek Singh Ahluwalia and N. K. Singh handle delicate issues like securing more assistance with fewer strings attached. Soon the process of liberalisation and the tenets of a free-market economy began to make itself felt in the way India did business. The Embassy went from being a facilitator of aid to a promoter of investments. Shringla was at the thick of this, working with some of the largest French firms such as Elf Aquitaine, Total, Snecma and Air Liquide in this endeavour. Shringla worked hard to ensure that every query by an Indian exporter was responded to and that meticulous preparations for every commercial event in France were made to present the best opportunities to our exporters. His long hours of work were noticed by all at the embassy, and some of his staff referred to him as a "workaholic". Perhaps the plethora of delegations that visited Paris in those days and the increasing workload that found its way onto his desk did not give him the adequate appreciation of one of the most exciting world capitals.

Harsh Shringla made it a point to constantly learn and better himself, although not always in a planned or conscious manner. He strove to imbibe best practices from his seniors and contemporaries. In this endeavour, he had excellent role models in the two Ambassadors he worked under. C. V. Ranganathan, an erudite and accomplished diplomat, a China expert and former Ambassador to China, who found himself somewhat out of place in France, and Ranjit Sethi, perhaps the best linguist the service has ever produced. Both Ambassadors, especially Sethi, worked closely with Shringla even though he was relatively junior in the hierarchy. Mr. Shringla recalls Sethi's immaculate use of the French language and his sophisticated disposition. He also learnt from other senior officers such as Rajiv and Veena Sikri and Sunder Sharma and continues to maintain contact with them.

Shringla made friends in each of his postings. He met one of his closest friends, Laurent Collet, on a flight out of Paris. His friendships with Sri Lankans Iswaran Natarajan or Ish and Prithviraj Pereira or Prithi endured over time and they continue to remain in touch. Shringla remembers with some regret that he could not maintain contact with one of his friends from his first posting in Paris, Shankar, a unique individual who lived life on his own uncompromising terms. Shankar was a self-made man. Highly learned and intelligent, Shankar travelled from India to Iran where he was offered a job by famous photographer Roloff Beny. He made enough money in those days to continue his travels to Europe. One day while hitchhiking, he met with a serious accident that sent him into a coma and created health complications for him from which he never truly recovered. In Paris, he was employed by UNESCO and worked with this international organisation for several years until his uncompromising attitude got him fired. In this second term, Shringla tried to help Shankar to the extent that he could, including finding him employment in the embassy. Shankar lived in a one-room tenement in Paris but could prepare the most delicious vegetarian meals with a running commentary of classical music. Shankar was like a walking encyclopaedia. Shringla recalls Shankar's depth of knowledge on practically any subject under the sun. One day, Shringla was asked by an acquaintance to procure a certain product he had never heard of. He decided to test Shankar by asking him about this. Shankar not only knew that this was a banned substance used at horse races but strongly advised him not to have anything to do with it!

At the end of his term, Shringla was replaced by his good friend, Sandeep Kumar, who also continued to occupy the apartment at Rue Saint-Saëns near the Eiffel Tower, traditionally reserved for the commercial officers of the embassy.

5

MID LEVEL IFS

ON COMPLETION of his posting to Paris, Harsh Shringla returned to New Delhi in 1995 for a posting at the Ministry's headquarters. His first posting was in the Europe West Division as Deputy Secretary. Europe West is considered to be one of the "heaviest" territorial divisions in the Ministry and is assigned the task of managing India's relations with major European countries such as the United Kingdom, France, Germany, Netherlands, Italy and also with the European Union and, in his time, with the Commonwealth.

This was his first experience of working at a "desk" in the Ministry of External Affairs. This is a job where officers back from their first stints abroad work the nuts and bolts of the Indian diplomatic operation. Desk officers are the go-to persons in any bilateral relationship. They are the "hands-on" officers involved in the day-to-day issues that are the staple of diplomacy. Shringla learned the basics of the desk job here. Processing the inputs from Indian missions from abroad and converting them into briefs on various issues; interacting with foreign missions in Delhi; attending meetings and calls, and basic administrative tasks.

Those who worked with Shringla at that time recall that although a Deputy Secretary, Shringla was the de facto Director of the Division with an independent office. He was fortunate to have as his boss Joint Secretary S. (Shatto) Pal, one of the brightest officers of the service. Shatto was an officer who believed in supporting those who worked. He gave Shringla full freedom in his functioning and was generous in nominating him for those visits that gave him the greatest exposure. Shringla recalls that one of his daily chores was to facilitate visas to a long list of referred cases. Here again, his organisational skills came into best use and Shringla soon worked out a modus vivendi with his European embassy counterparts that produced the best results for all. He would share a list every morning on the basis of full disclosure and his counterpart would revert by the evening with most cases accepted and with reasons for those that were not.

Shringla was promoted as Director in the Ministry of External Affairs in May 1997 and was then appointed as Director (North). This marked a significant increase in responsibilities. Over the next decade, Shringla would hone his professional skills, be entrusted with increasingly complex and important assignments, and significantly expand his repertoire of diplomatic knowledge. He would move from being Director (North) in the Ministry of External Affairs to being second in command, as Deputy Chief of Mission at the Embassy of India in Tel Aviv, to serving in one of India's most prestigious missions, the Permanent Mission of India to the United Nations in New York, and finally to South Africa as Consul General of India in Durban.

Each assignment was a step up. All of them were extremely "sought-after" jobs. With each move, he acquired a "track record" and demonstrated that he was on an upward trajectory and that he had been marked out as an officer of unusual promise and ability.

The Northern Division of the Ministry is one of its oldest territorial units and oversees the diplomatic relationship with Nepal and Bhutan. The diplomatic equations with these two countries—though very different in many respects—are amongst the most important that India has. The neighbourhood is India's primary diplomatic arena. In a speech that he made decades later as Foreign Secretary, Harsh Shringla would say that, "The countries in our neighbourhood are of unique and special strategic significance to India, both because they are deeply interconnected with us through ties of geography, culture and history, and also because the internal and external dimensions of our policy—and theirs—intersect and overlap with each other. Relations with them also impact our own states that border these neighbours. Accordingly, the neighbourhood remains our primary diplomatic arena. It is first and foremost among our foreign policy priorities. The primacy given to the neighbourhood in our diplomatic efforts is reflected in our Neighbourhood First policy."

This was Shringla's first exposure to the neighbourhood. The position of Director (North) is considered to be one of the most difficult jobs at that level. It is assigned to those who have established their reputations as hard-working officers. The relationship with Nepal and Bhutan has a major and very sensitive political dimension. Relations with Nepal, which has historically had a more volatile polity than Bhutan, have tested the skills of some of India's greatest diplomats. Proximity produces stress and complications. It involves borders and movements of people and of goods and services. It involves inter-agency processes and commands the attention of the highest levels of government. It also has significant economic dimensions. India's development partnership programme, now a full-fledged agency with a billion dollar portfolio, began with projects in Nepal and Bhutan.

Harsh Shringla worked in the North Division at a very interesting time. Prime Minister (and External Affairs Minister) I. K. Gujral, had just introduced a set of policies that were later described as the Gujral Doctrine. He himself described one of its fundamental tenets states as "with its neighbours like Bangladesh, Bhutan, Maldives, Nepal, and Sri Lanka, India does not ask for reciprocity, but gives and accommodates what it can in good faith and trust." Shringla, therefore, started his work in the neighbourhood during a transformative period. The influence of this period can be detected in his actions and priorities as he rose through the ranks to be one of the most experienced officers in dealing with the neighbourhood.

India's relations with Nepal and Bhutan saw major changes during this period. The ratification of the Mahakali Treaty in June 1997 added a new dimension to India-Nepal relations. India accepted Nepal's request for an additional transit route to Bangladesh via Fulbari. India also began funding mega power projects in Bhutan which later became a model for regional arrangements in energy cooperation.

Shringla was fortunate here also in having as his Joint Secretary, Sudhir Vyas who had tremendous knowledge and interest in the history and politics of Nepal and Bhutan. An avid ornithologist in his spare time, Vyas believed extensive travel in-country was the best way of developing an understanding of these two key neighbours. Shringla recalls driving from the border with Bhutan at Phuentsholing all the way to Bhutan's borders with Tibet at Haa. In fact, on a separate journey, Shringla had just reached Thimphu when he received news of the birth of his son, Ashoka in Mumbai. He had to rush back through a circuitous route via Calcutta. In Nepal, Shringla oversaw the construction of the 22-bridges project along the East-West highway in Nepal's Terai region running parallel to India. It reminded him of the drive he and his brother had undertaken many years earlier on this flat stretch of road on return from Kathmandu to Darjeeling.

ISRAEL

Harsh Shringla was then posted to the Embassy of India in Tel Aviv. India's relations with Israel stand out as a very special case. India opened its Embassy in Tel Aviv as recently as 1992. The relations with Israel in the last two decades have become one of India's most dynamic and substantive. Israel and India today have excellent political contacts, a very important strategic partnership with major exchanges in defence, counterterrorism, and critical technologies, growing people-to-people contacts, and a very forward-looking economic partnership.

This was not the case when Shringla reached there. He was therefore one of the pioneers. It was also further recognition of his professional standing as an officer who could be entrusted with a challenging task. He served there under Ambassador Ranjan Mathai, who would later rise to become Foreign Secretary. Ambassador Mathai succeeded Ambassador Shiv Shankar Menon who too would become Foreign Secretary. The assignment to Israel was therefore a prestigious one.

Shringla's tenure in Israel saw the foundations of the current relationship being laid. There were multiple Ministerial and other high-level visits during this period which served as a platform for deeper engagement between New Delhi and Tel Aviv. In 2000, the then Minister of External Affairs, Jaswant Singh visited Israel. This was the first such visit by the Minister of External Affairs of India since the establishment of Embassies in 1992. In the same year, Home Minister L. K. Advani paid a 4-day visit to Israel. Among other visitors were the then Communications Minister, Pramod Mahajan and West Bengal Chief Minister, Jyoti Basu.

There were tangible outcomes to these state visits in the form of MoUs on cooperation in Industrial Research and Development, setting up of working groups on issues such as counterterrorism, and setting up of a Ministerial level Joint Commission with a view to developing a long-term framework for cooperation. This era also saw the emergence of people-to-people ties with broader engagement between civil society actors. All of these marked a deepening of ties during the era.

Shringla, who was Counsellor (Commerce) at the Embassy, also made a mark as an economic diplomat. One of his important accomplishments was the execution of Project Granite at the New Ben Gurion International Airport. He played a major role in supplying granite from India and worked closely with the Indian suppliers, Chemicals and Allied Products Export Promotion Council of India (CAPEXIL), the Israeli importer, and the Israel-Asia Chamber of Commerce during the project. This project involved entry into a relatively new but highly developed market where India's economic capabilities had not been fully demonstrated.

There were initiatives such as the India exclusive Trade Exhibition being held in Tel Aviv. Held in May 2000, about a year after his arrival, it was the very first exhibition and conference of its kind in which 115 companies from India from various sectors, such as textiles, handicrafts, home equipment, gift items, gems and jewellery participated. A novelty at that time—much before the Indian auto industry came into its own—was the automotive presence which showcased a Tata pickup truck.

As Counsellor (Commercial), Shringla organised this in cooperation with the India Trade Promotion Organisation (ITPO), Delhi. ITPO coordinated the Indian end of the exhibition and was instrumental in organising an impressive number of manufacturers and tradespeople from all across India to participate in the event and display their wares. Shringla himself reached out to a number of organisations in India.

Shringla's team at the Embassy worked with a number of service providers on complex preparations for this event. It involved interaction with participating companies—most of whom were completely new to Israel—including helping them with local logistics such as accommodation and transportation. It also involved connecting with a large number of Israeli companies, promoting the event, and working with various contractors.

An exhibition was held at the sprawling Tel Aviv Fairground which attracted an estimated 55,000 Israelis. It generated tremendous interest among Israeli consumers—commercial companies, tradespeople and the buying public. They saw the products, interacted with the exhibitors and participated in a large number of seminars and conferences that were hosted by various Indian organisations. The seminars were on general subjects such as "Doing Business in India" or on specific sectors such as Textiles and Footwear. For many Israelis and Israeli companies, this was the first exposure to the commercial potential of the Indian market and its strengths and opportunities in sectors as diverse as agriculture, manufacturing, pharmaceuticals, IT, and outsourcing services.

The exhibition had a segment on Yoga and Ayurvedic treatments that proved to be extremely popular. A special booth managed by an India-trained Ayurvedic Doctor offered ayurvedic massage treatment free-of-cost. Over 500 patients visited the booth. Indian food and tea were also featured. The Tea Board of India was at hand to offer Indian teas to visitors to the Exhibition. Internationally acclaimed fashion designer, Ms. Ritu Kumar organised a fashion show. The events were widely covered by Israeli and Indian media.

What Harsh Shringla's team remembers from that time was how he was in complete command of these activities and how he led with the utmost calm and professionalism. The patterns that marked him out in future diplomatic postings were beginning to emerge. He was a team player who had a combination of human qualities and professional competence. His temperament, controlled discipline, dynamism, and ability to think on his feet and take quick and decisive action also made a mark on those who worked and interacted with him. His ability to inspire loyalty among those who worked for him also became apparent. They experienced both his professional excellence and a very kind and warm individual who created a pleasant and caring work environment. He proved to be extremely popular with the Indian origin Israeli community, attending their events and interacting with them frequently. His sports loving nature is also remembered as is his setting up a hockey club in Israel.

After completing his tenure in Tel Aviv, he was posted as Minister at the Permanent Mission of India to the United Nations in New York. He served there from July 2002 to August 2006. New York is often described as the diplomatic capital of the world. The United Nations is headquartered there. The Security Council and the General Assembly meet there. The Secretary General who heads the UN Secretariat is also based in New York. The annual United Nations General Assembly, usually held in September, is one of the world's major diplomatic events.

NEW YORK

The Permanent Mission of India to the United Nations in New York is considered by many to be India's flagship diplomatic mission. Many also consider it to be one of India's best repositories of diplomatic talent. A posting to that mission is highly prized and is considered to be a confirmation that the officer is on the "fast track". Heads of that Mission include such luminaries as Shri Hamid Ansari, later Vice President of India; Ambassador Kamalesh Sharma, later Commonwealth Secretary General; and Shri Hardeep Puri, later a Union Minister.

India has a long and distinguished record at the United Nations. It was one of the leaders of the Non-Aligned Movement and of the Group of 77. India's position in the United Nations and in the multilateral world was however changing. India had acquired a reputation for being a voice for the developing world in the United Nations. It had been a leader on issues such as decolonisation, apartheid and peacekeeping.

India itself was changing. Economic reforms and investments in social capital produced sustained economic growth and an increase in capacities. India was seen as being on the cusp of major power status. This found reflection in India's interest in the UN Security Council and its campaign to acquire permanent member status. During his tenure in New York, he focused on this Security Council portfolio. He covered items on the Security Council agenda such as terrorism, Afghanistan, the Middle East and the Iraq war.

He did not know it then but this stint was the foundation of a long and distinguished career as a multilateralist. He would head the Ministry's UN Political Division when India joined the Security Council after a two-decade-long hiatus in 2011. He would also be Foreign Secretary when India next joined the Security Council in 2021. Shringla started his career working at UNESCO in Paris and later represented India at UN ESCAP in Bangkok.

Shringla's diplomatic reporting—the core professional competence of a foreign service officer—is remembered by those who read it. Although not a member of the Security Council, Mr. Shringla had an uncanny ability to befriend colleagues from other countries who were on the Council. He was thus one of the best-informed diplomats in his beat and was able to provide timely and accurate information and insights. His French colleague, who later became France's Ambassador to India, called him one of the finest diplomats in the UN. The Security Council is the diplomatic high table of the world and discusses issues of great complexity and weight. It was not enough to be well-informed. One required political insight and even sagacity. A feel for the ebb and flow of power and the nature of the interaction between great and major powers was also necessary. Shringla's reporting attracted attention and filtered up the system in India because of this combination of insight and information.

The UN Security Council was exceptionally active during this period. Its agenda had a strong African focus with Sudan, Burundi, the Democratic Republic of Congo, Liberia, Western Sahara, Ivory Coast, Somalia, Sierra Leone, Eritrea and Ethiopia figuring in it. This was also the period when a massive growth in UN Peacekeeping operations mandated by the Security Council was acquiring strength and led to the creation of the UN Peacebuilding Commission in 2005. The so-called multidimensional, or complex peacekeeping operations, in which India was becoming a major contributor were unfolding. Concepts such as "peace-building" and the discourse on "failed states" were gathering momentum. The historic World Summit of 2005 which among other things endorsed the path-breaking legal concept of the Responsibility to Protect also happened during this period.

Shringla had his hands full in tracking and reporting on all of these issues and more. The situation in the Middle East, and in particular, Iraq, were also the centre stage on the United Nations agenda. Iraq was under United Nations sanctions. Shringla was the point man for monitoring and tracking the Security Council's involvement in Iraq. He faced an unusual challenge in 2005. He was able to obtain the findings of the Independent Inquiry Committee which probed into massive bribery in Iraq's "Oil for Food" programme, before the 1,000-word report was delivered to the Security Council, because of his considerable contacts in New York. K. Natwar Singh, the foreign affairs minister, was identified in the report, and he alerted his boss, Ambassador Nirupama Sen, Permanent Representative to the United Nations. No one in the diplomatic mission, other than these two men, had any inkling of what was to come. Shringla was cool, controlled, and collected when a journalist acquaintance saw him at the UN that day, and there was no sign that this diplomat possessed material that would inflame India's politics in a day or two. Mr. Sen was able to bypass the Ministry of External Affairs (MEA) and provide the damaging material directly to Prime Minister Manmohan Singh. After a failed resistance, Mr. Natwar Singh resigned.

Shringla's tenure in New York was in a sense the completion of one segment of his diplomatic life. He had acquired an understanding of the most rapidly growing branch of diplomatic business, the world of multilateral and plurilateral diplomacy. He had acquired a knowledge of the Security Council and its methods. He had been involved in the complex negotiations of the Non-Aligned Movement and participated in their summits. He had also worked on the front lines of the campaign for a permanent seat in the UN Security Council. This was to prove useful to him as he ascended the IFS ladder, and provided the foundation for a rare blend of bilateral and multilateral experience.

DURBAN

After a successful tenure in New York, it was time for Harsh Shringla to move further up the ladder of professional responsibility. Like many "high-fliers", he was assigned to head one of India's important medium-sized diplomatic outposts. He would once again fly the flag as India's Consul General in Durban in South Africa.

As in the case of Israel, Shringla was assigned to a challenging location where he would have an opportunity to build the foundations of the relationship between post-apartheid South Africa and India. South Africa is a country with which India has an extraordinary relationship. It is home to one of the largest populations of people of Indian descent in Africa. More than a million Indian-origin South Africans have made that country home. Most of them reside around Durban which is sometimes called the "largest Indian city outside India". India's cultural heritage is intricately woven into the fabric of the great city of Durban and is reflected in the city's architecture and cultural outlook.

Shringla served as the Consul General of India in Durban from August 2006 to December 2009. He began his tenure by managing the historic visit of Prime Minister Manmohan Singh to South Africa, including a two-day Durban trip, within a few weeks of his taking over. Prime Minister Singh's visit to Durban commemorated the joint celebration of the centenary of Satyagraha, which Mahatma Gandhi had launched, in Johannesburg on September 11, 1906. A Tshwane Declaration was signed that reaffirmed and deepened the strategic partnership between India and South Africa and laid down benchmarks in numerous areas of cooperation including health, science & technology, trade & investment, defence, culture, education, and atomic energy.

Diaspora diplomacy had not yet acquired the salience it would in the later years. Indian diplomats and missions and posts had not yet acquired the reputation for connecting and responding to the diaspora that they were to acquire in the future. Shringla's tenure in Durban exposed him to and allowed him to acquire a grasp of the nature of consular operations and diaspora-related diplomatic work amongst one of the largest concentrations of Indians outside India. This would stand him in good stead more than a decade later when he was to preside over one of India's largest and most successful diaspora diplomacy operations as Ambassador of India to the United States, and still later as Foreign Secretary, when he would run one of the world's largest consular operations.

He earned a reputation for being an accessible and friendly diplomat with a large following in Durban and its surrounding areas. People remember that he undertook a number of activities that encouraged social cohesion between communities living in this part of South Africa. He became an effective public speaker, able to articulate the progressive thinking underlying the Indian nation-building experience, and became a celebrity who was always in demand for events.

The Consulate also became a hub of cultural activity that promoted the linguistic and cultural links between the diaspora and India. Local Indian-origin South Africans felt that he had personally helped many with whom he interacted to appreciate the deep Indian influence on their ideals and their morals. He was able to kindle pride in India, in being Indian and in Indian traditions such as inclusiveness and tolerance. His national day events, such as Republic Day, were much-anticipated and became focal points for the community.

Harsh Shringla was one of the earlier Indian Consuls General in Durban. As in the case of Israel, Indians in that area remember him with a great deal of affection and respect. A large number of them continue to follow him on social media and cheer him for his successes. Speaking of his enduring connection with people from that region, one of them said that, "As busy as he is in his life in the political stratosphere you can count on a special birthday greeting from Mr. Shringla without prejudice of who you are and this shows his amazing grace as a human being."

A perceptive observer also noted another quality about Harsh Shringla. He was a gentleman with a strong sense of honour and integrity. They also noted his devotion to his parents and how much of an influence they had on him. An interlocutor remarks that one of her "most treasured memories was having breakfast with both his parents in his official residence which was such an honour and pleasure because I found that he had an exemplary set of parents which led to his honourable stature in society."

Another Mr. Shringla quality was also becoming apparent—an excellent memory and an ability to listen. A friend from that period observed that "he remembers every conversation he has had with you and recalls names of people you may have mentioned which adds to a relationship with someone."

This was his second stint as Consul General after his posting as head of the post in Ho Chi Minh City a decade earlier. This was, however, his first major "independent charge". It demonstrated that Harsh Shringla was creating his own distinctive style of diplomacy. Accessible, articulate, professionally competent, innovative and above all, a people's man with an unparalleled ability to make friends and connect with them.

6

JOINT SECRETARY

THE JOB of the Joint Secretary in the Ministry of External Affairs is often described as the "cutting edge" of the Ministry. Joint Secretaries head the Divisions with territorial or topical jurisdiction that handle all diplomatic work. They formulate policy, execute decisions, coordinate inter-agency processes, interact with foreign missions in Delhi and supervise the diplomatic operations of Indian missions abroad.

There is, naturally, a hierarchy or pecking order among Divisions in the Ministry of External Affairs. The Ministry's organogram on its website lists about 40 Divisions. A closer examination reveals that only a few of them report to the Foreign Secretary. The rest report to other Secretaries. It can therefore be assumed that all Joint Secretaries are not equal. Those who report to the Foreign Secretary must be higher on the pecking order.

Broadly speaking, these are Divisions that manage India's relations with its neighbourhood and major partners such as the USA, UK, France, Germany, Russia, China and Japan.

Harsh Shringla was Joint Secretary at the Ministry of External Affairs Headquarters from 2010 to 2013. During this period, he first headed the SAARC Division, then the UN Political Division and finally the BSM (Bangladesh, Sri Lanka, Myanmar, Maldives) Division. In all these assignments, Shringla reported to the Foreign Secretary and handled some of India's key diplomatic accounts.

SAARC

As Joint Secretary of SAARC, he was the point person for all matters concerning the South Asian Association for Regional Cooperation. This division manages a complicated diplomatic equation in which South Asian neighbours in India's immediate neighbourhood have attempted with varying degrees of success to create a regional organisation known as SAARC. SAARC has succeeded in creating a number of institutions and understandings in spite of the often-bitter political debates and disagreements. SAARC, as an organisation, during that period, in the words of the Ministry's Annual Report (2009-2010) saw a "gradual and irreversible transition" from the "declaratory to the implementation phase".

The 16th SAARC Summit, held in Thimphu, from April 28-29, 2010, has been described as a historic event, coinciding as it did with the 25th Anniversary Year of SAARC. It was addressed by Prime Minister Manmohan Singh. Shringla worked closely with Foreign Secretary Nirupama Rao on the theme of the Summit which was on Climate Change, and helped draft the SAARC Thimphu Silver Jubilee Declaration entitled "Towards a Green and Happy South Asia" and a separate Ministerial Statement on Climate Change that was adopted at the Summit.

This was also the period when the groundwork for one of SAARC's most important projects, the South Asian University in Delhi, was done. Pakistan used the SAARC consensus-based decision-making process to its advantage to stymie any Indian initiative. Recognising Dr. Manmohan Singh's personal interest in the South Asian University, Pakistan's focus was on keeping this prestigious project from receiving the endorsement of the Summit. Shringla had to use all of his interpersonal and negotiating skills to see this through. He was especially appreciative of the Bhutanese hosts for the fullest support they extended in seeing India's endeavours at SAARC succeed.

As such, during his tenure in the SAARC Division, Shringla was able to demonstrate his ability to navigate the complex terrain of South Asian diplomatic politics. He also demonstrated a problem-solving ability and focused on the implementation of concrete projects. It gave him a solid understanding of the complications of the issues related to the implementation of projects which were to form an important component of the Neighbourhood First policy.

UNITED NATIONS POLITICAL

Harsh Shringla was then moved to the United Nations Political Division or the UNP Division of the Ministry. This Division is the heart of the Indian multilateral diplomatic machinery and has an extensive charter of duties that relate to the United Nations, the Non-Aligned Movement, India's campaign for a permanent UN Security Council seat, United Nations peacekeeping operations, and anti-piracy operations in the Indian Ocean, amongst other things. It is also the division that is most closely associated with the Permanent Mission of India to the United Nations in New York. His appointment to this job therefore marked, in a sense, a homecoming for Shringla and also a recognition of his skills as a multilateral diplomat. Multilateralists are something of a specialisation within the Indian Foreign Service and with his appointment as Joint Secretary UNP, he was established as an officer with very high levels of expertise and competence in this arena.

His appointment was important for another reason. This was the year in which India fought a fierce campaign for a non-permanent seat in the UN Security Council. Its last tenure as a non-permanent member was in 1991-1992. It had tried to win a seat in 1994 but lost rather ignominiously to Japan. It did not even make the second round of voting and the loss of Shri Shashi Tharoor in the United Nations Secretary General's elections in 2006 scarred India's diplomatic psyche.

Shringla's tenure at the UNP Division saw a reversal of these defeats. Working closely with India's Permanent Representative to the United Nations in New York, Ambassador Hardeep Singh Puri, he played a key role in ensuring a resounding victory winning 184 out of 192 votes, the highest among candidates for election as non-permanent members to the UN Security Council. Ambassador Hardeep Singh Puri, one of the best known and respected officers of the IFS, went on to become Union Minister. At the time of writing this book, India is once again in the United Nations Security Council for another non-permanent tenure. In a remarkable turn of the wheel of fate, Shringla became Foreign Secretary and Hardeep Singh Puri is serving as Union Minister.

India joined the United Nations Security Council after a two-decades-long wait on January 1, 2011. The Security Council is at the high table of international diplomacy. The five permanent members of the Council are entrusted with the responsibility of maintaining international peace and security. The Council is seized of some of the most pressing and immediate problems of the day. It is also an arena where great power politics can be witnessed in its most direct and elemental forms. The Joint Secretary UNP was the point person in the Ministry and now had the responsibility of ensuring that India was prepared to deal with the responsibility of becoming a non-permanent member after a two-decades-long hiatus. When India joined the Council on January 1, 2011, Joint Secretary of UNP was the coordinator in the Government of India for ensuring that India's participation in the Security Council and its momentous proceedings and decisions were informed and calculated decisions. He was responsible for "backstopping" India's participation in the Council's proceedings. It has to be kept in mind that India was not an "ordinary" non-permanent member. It was an aspiring permanent member of the Security Council. Its participation and contributions were, therefore, subject to careful scrutiny and examination by the international community and in the domestic arena.

The year 2011 was a momentous year in international politics. One of the first decisions that the Indian delegation took as a member of the Security Council in January 2011 was to vote for the closure of the UN Mission in Nepal (UNMIN), with which New Delhi had its misgivings. The Council continued to deal with its routine business of international peace through its agenda which had a heavy focus on conflict prevention, peacekeeping and peacebuilding, particularly in Africa. This was soon interrupted by two conflicts which continue to haunt India to this day. These are the internal conflicts in Syria and Libya. The question of whether to intervene or not in these essentially international conflicts—both of which exerted a heavy humanitarian toll on civilians—was one of the most vexed diplomatic questions of the day. At one end, India was required to navigate the diplomatic and ethical questions that relate to humanitarian distress. At another end were the imperatives of sovereignty and the effectiveness of coercive options such as military interventions.

BSM (BANGLADESH-SRI LANKA-MYANMAR-MALDIVES)

Harsh Shringla's career was set to take off while he wrestled with these challenging concerns. When India was contracted to build 50,000 houses in civil war-ravaged Tamil areas through a line of credit to Sri Lanka in 2011, a civil war erupted within the MEA, with the Joint

Secretary in charge of Sri Lanka accusing the then External Affairs Minister, S. M. Krishna's office of contract corruption on file. The IFS officer and the minister's office were fighting an unequal struggle, but the Joint Secretary dug in his heels, even refusing an ambassadorial assignment to stay on and fight alleged political corruption.

For the then Foreign Secretary Nirupama Rao, this situation could not be sustained. The compromise was to draft Harsh Shringla as Joint Secretary for Sri Lanka, who firmly, but diplomatically ended the civil war within the Ministry and successfully oversaw the completion of the housing projects sans any corruption. This experience stood him in good stead later in delivering critical assistance to Bangladesh, as High Commissioner, making relations with Dhaka one of the recent success stories of the Narendra Modi government's neighbourhood diplomacy.

As Joint Secretary UNP, Shringla dealt with the Permanent Mission of India to the United Nations in New York. As Joint Secretary BSM he coordinated with four of India's most important missions—Dhaka, Colombo, Yangon and Male—and with the Ambassador and High Commissioners of Bangladesh, Sri Lanka, Myanmar and Maldives in New Delhi. Indian Embassies and High Commissions to neighbouring countries have traditionally been staffed by the best Indian diplomatic talent. Indian Ambassadors and High Commissioners in neighbouring countries are usually among the most respected and able Indian diplomats.

These are also unusually complex diplomatic accounts dealing with the entire range of relations with these countries. Politics, history, contemporary realities, economic imperatives, shared heritage and cultures, contested histories and old problems combine with each other to produce difficult diplomatic problems. There is also an element of volatility that often makes the unexpected something of an everyday occurrence in these diplomatic accounts.

Harsh Shringla earned the confidence of Foreign Secretaries Nirupama Rao and Ranjan Mathai through his work on Sri Lankan housing and other major projects that the Division then directly dealt with. He went on to more than repay the confidence they reposed in him through several major policies and operational successes over the next two years.

As Joint Secretary BSM, Shringla operated on a vast canvas. The geographical spread of his responsibilities extended from South East Asia to the Indian Ocean. We can, however, focus on some key highlights of his tenure.

Bangladesh at that time had witnessed the return of Sheikh Hasina to power after a spell of Army rule. Army rule followed after the Prime Ministership of Begum Khaleda Zia and a government (2001-2006) with a Bangladesh Nationalist Party (BNP) majority. A number of irritants had arisen in bilateral relations during that period. These included slow movement on several bilateral issues such as the border, concerns about Indian insurgent groups in Bangladesh and trade tensions. Much work was done by Shringla during that time to reduce tensions in bilateral relations and then place it on a trajectory that would make it a remarkable turnaround story in Shringla's subsequent tenure as High Commissioner.

The political situation in Bangladesh, although stable, was marked by violence as Bangladesh went through a series of war crimes tribunals. The protocol to the Land Boundary Agreement (LBA) signed in 2011 and ratified in 2015, could perhaps be considered one of the most significant achievements in the recent history of India-Bangladesh relations. It was like the 1996 Treaty between India and Bangladesh *On Sharing of the Ganges Waters at Farakka*, a defining agreement between these two countries. The LBA Protocol, however, involved more stakeholders at both the central and state levels and called for correspondingly greater consultation and coordination. It also required a special effort to develop a new approach that was shared by all parties to old problems.

There had been serious efforts in the past to arrive at a comprehensive settlement of the land boundary between India and Bangladesh (erstwhile

East Pakistan) since 1947. The Nehru-Noon agreement of 1958 and 1974 LBA (India Bangladesh Land Boundary Agreement) was unable to address three difficult issues—the undemarcated land boundary of approximately 6.1 km, the exchange of enclaves and adverse possessions that remained unsettled. For a variety of reasons, including the lack of political will, these issues remain unresolved.

By the time this complicated issue landed on Shringla's plate, the political dynamics had changed. There was a desire to improve relations with Bangladesh. Shringla capitalised on this factor which is, however, a necessary but not sufficient precondition. True to his character, he came up with a pragmatic effort that considered the ground situation and the wishes of the people residing in the areas. He also developed the agreement with the full support and concurrence of the State governments concerned (Assam, Meghalaya, Tripura and West Bengal).

This called for elaborate planning, extensive consultation with people in the border areas involved, and multiple visits by joint India-Bangladesh delegations to enclaves and adverse possessions with the final aim of ensuring that the interests of the people on the two sides were protected. The 2011 protocol departed from the 1974 LBA in seeking to maintain the status quo of adverse possessions instead of the exchange territories in deference to the wishes of the people to remain in their land.

He and his team made several visits to the borders to obtain a ground view of the situation. Some of these areas had never been previously visited by a Government of India representative. Some of his colleagues recall Harsh Shringla walking through miles of paddy files and traversing rivers to reach inaccessible areas of the border. He was astute in the manner in which he involved the state governments. He understood that their concurrence was not only required to take the deal through but also to deal with possible political opposition. He consulted them widely and frequently and brought them on board. Similarly, he negotiated with skill and understanding with the Bangladeshi side.

His visits had given him a solid understanding of the situation on the ground. Armed with this knowledge, and his diplomatic skills, he was able to convince all parties on both sides that a pragmatic solution was necessary for the interests of both countries and also of the states. His idea of a joint India-Bangladesh survey to ascertain the wishes of the people increased mutual confidence and demonstrated that the people on the ground actually wanted to minimise dislocation. Ultimately, all stakeholders in governments on both sides and political parties accepted this formula. The result was a breakthrough agreement that removed a major irritant in bilateral relations and cleared the way for much greater cooperation. The 1974 India-Bangladesh Land Boundary Agreement came into force on June 6, 2015, after Prime Minister Narendra Modi of India and Prime Minister Sheikh Hasina of Bangladesh exchanged ratification instruments during Prime Minister Modi's State visit to Bangladesh. The agreement calls for the exchange of pockets of Indian and Bangladeshi territory, as well as the clarification of the India-Bangladesh border, which has been a source of contention since the 1947 partition.

One of Harsh Shringla's colleagues who worked in the BSM Division at that time remarked, "the officer who played a very crucial role in this, and was in fact the linchpin, right from the drafting of the protocol, to its signing stage, was Shri Harsh Vardhan Shringla."

Myanmar witnessed a period of rare political consolidation that culminated in the election of Aung San Suu Kyi (DASSK) as Prime Minister later in 2015. The beginnings of political activity and a degree of openness were however evident and Prime Minister Manmohan Singh paid an official visit to Myanmar, the first such visit by an Indian Prime Minister to Myanmar since 1987. Shringla implemented a remarkable plan to support Myanmar's nascent democracy through capacity-building programmes on federalism and parliamentary procedures for officials of Myanmar's fledgling parliament and democratic institutions. In the first of his many meeting with DASSK in April 2011, he accompanied Foreign Secretary Nirupama Rao to DASSK's iconic house on the shores of Inlay Lake where she was under house arrest. This was the first contact between a representative of the Indian Government and DASSK for a significant period of time.

This was also a period that saw a transformational approach toward improving connectivity and development partnerships in these countries. With regard to Sri Lanka, the Ministry of External Affairs Annual Report of 2012-13, states that "India is involved in the rehabilitation and resettlement efforts of Internally Displaced Persons (IDPs) and the reconstruction process in Northern and Eastern Sri Lanka. India's assistance in Sri Lanka, in the areas of housing, demining, education, public health, connectivity and culture, has been a part of these efforts. The Government of India project to build 50,000 houses for IDPs in Sri Lanka is under implementation. A Pilot Project involving the construction of 1,000 houses was successfully completed in July 2012. The second phase of the housing project (for the remaining 49,000 houses) was launched in all five districts of the Northern Province of Sri Lanka on October 2, 2012 and completed in 2018. The third phase of the Indian Housing Project involved the construction of 4,000 houses for estate workers in the Central and Uva Provinces through an innovative community-driven approach. Letter of Exchange with the Government of Sri Lanka for this phase was signed in April 2016 and work started in October 2016. However, as Foreign Secretary on October 4, 2021, Shringla got the opportunity to hand over more than 1,200 houses constructed as part of its development efforts in Sri Lanka. While jointly inaugurating 4 projects in the housing and education sectors with Hon'ble Sri Lankan Foreign Minister, Prof. G. L. Peiris, in the presence of several Cabinet Ministers and MPs, Shringla asserted that these projects, completed with Indian assistance, exemplify India's strong and multifaceted development cooperation profile in Sri Lanka.

The Government of India also undertook several infrastructure development projects in Northern Sri Lanka as part of the development assistance programme. These included the rehabilitation of the Kankesanthurai Harbour, the construction of a Cultural Centre in Jaffna and the construction of a 150-bed hospital in Dickoya. A Government of India Line of Credit of US$ 167.4 million to Sri Lanka has been used for the repair and upgradation of the Tsunami-damaged Colombo-Matara rail link.

Shringla also worked with the private sector which was on its own, and in partnership with the government, acquiring salience in the neighbourhood. One of the interesting cases that he worked on related to the GMR Group, a leading Indian infrastructure company, in a project relating to Malé airport. In the words of Arun Mubai, a top GMR executive: "GMR had won the World Bank led project for Malé airport in the Maldives and the job was to develop a new airport at Malé which started in 2012 and the work was in steady progress. Our credentials were perfectly honest and straight and effective. But through no fault of ours because of their political reasons, the Maldives government wanted us out. We were left with no option but to approach our own government for help in this matter and to request them to intervene. So, the matter had to be taken from government to government and that is how Harsh Shringla, who was the first step because he was the Joint Secretary, directly concerned in the Maldives, came into the picture. Through a series of meetings, we explained to him how we had won the airport bid in an international competition, and how this bidding process was led by IFC, which is a member of the World Bank Group. Mr. Shringla understood our position and dug deep into the matter and decided for himself that the matter was fair, and judged our credentials completely honest. He felt that an Indian company was not being treated correctly by the Maldives government and then took it up and escalated the matter."

The Maldives saw a period of intense political unrest during Shingla's tenure which required adroit Indian diplomacy. A constitutional crisis erupted on the island in 2011 with riots and a high level of political instability. As Joint Secretary BSM in the MEA looking after Bangladesh, Sri Lanka, Myanmar and Maldives, it was often the smallest and silent M in BSM that needed the most attention. In early February, President Mohamad Nasheed was deposed by what he termed a coup d'état by elements of the army, police and right-wing politicians of the country. President Nasheed, a UK-educated human rights activist, had spearheaded the pro-democracy movement that saw the end of erstwhile President Abdul Gayoom's hold over the country. The country witnessed a series of protests and demonstrations. The political polarisation threatened the very existence of this nascent democracy. Matters came to a head when Nasheed Suo Moto sought refuge in the Indian High Commission. The Maldivian Government reacted strongly, warning of direct intervention if Nasheed did not leave the diplomatic premises. Despite the best efforts of the Indian diplomatic establishment, the matter could not be resolved and Nasheed continued to remain at the High Commission. The Indian and international media started warming up to the story, one which seemed to suggest India's inability to deal effectively with a situation involving it in its own immediate neighbourhood. As a last recourse, Shringla was sent by External Affairs Minister Salman Khurshid and Foreign Secretary Mathai to do whatever it took to resolve an increasingly vexing issue. He found a complex and volatile situation when he arrived in Maldives and had to use every bit of his ingenuity and personal skills to unravel the real players that determined the outcome of the existing imbroglio. He was greatly helped by India's charismatic High Commissioner Dnyaneshwar Mulay, who found himself in an intractable and potentially embarrassing situation. We do not know all the details but Shringla's persistent efforts to ensure that the conditions for Nasheed's release, i.e. that he would not be arrested and not be barred from contesting the general elections, were agreed upon by Government. Ten days later, Nasheed stepped out of the High Commission to a tumultuous welcome by his supporters and Shringla could return home.

7

THAILAND

INDIA'S BILATERAL relations with Thailand are rooted in history, age-old social and cultural interactions and extensive people-to-people contact. India and Thailand, located in each other's extended neighbourhood, share a maritime boundary in the Andaman Sea. The shared link of Buddhism is reflected in regular pilgrimages to places of Buddhist interest in India by a large number of Thai people. Hindu elements can be found among those reflected in Thai architecture, arts, sculpture, dance, drama and literature—the Thai language incorporates Pali and Sanskrit influences. A large Indian diaspora living and working in Thailand is another important bond between these two nations.

Besides, both countries are important regional partners linking South and South-East Asia. They cooperate closely in the ASEAN,

East Asia Summit and BIMSTEC groupings as also Mekong Ganga Cooperation, Asia Cooperation Dialogue and Indian Ocean Rim Association.

As an ambassador to Thailand when the government changed hands in Delhi with Prime Minister Modi's government coming to power with an overwhelming majority, he never experienced this in recent Indian political history. Shringla had started studying Prime Minister Modi as a man and often contemplated his strong points as a leader of a nation and what his vision would be for a rising India and how he would lead the nation forward, especially with concern to international relations. Within the first few days of Prime Minister Modi coming to power, Shringla went on Thai television, one of the most popular channels in Thailand and with his in-depth understanding and observation he asserted that India with a new government headed by Prime Minister Modi had a very different outlook—a government that wanted accountability and expected everybody to deliver and wanted those in government to serve the people. This message was especially relevant to those who represented the country abroad.

The Indian diaspora became conspicuously important for the new Government in Delhi looking after the interests of its citizens. The general approach of many changed from being indifferent to being extremely attentive to what was required by overseas Indians. One of the first things Shringla initiated was to declare an Open House for anyone with a grievance for immediate redressal. He did this despite encountering resistance from within the embassy, as one faces challenges when trying to bring changes in the bureaucracy. The Open House would operate from 9 a.m. to 10 a.m. so that the common people who needed help and assistance would just drop by the Indian embassy with any issues or concerns or with their grievances. Shringla and his officers were very active during this early hour to address the issues faced by the Indian people in Thailand. In fact, the Open House could be equally accessed by

Thai people or, for that matter, anyone residing in Thailand facing issues with regard to passport, visa or getting certificate or any consular issue. He would try to sort it out in one window.

Harsh Shringla effortlessly connected with people; anyone could reach out to him. He never considered himself to be that distant figure and established a direct connection with people across communities. There were different sections of the Indian community coming from different parts of India with diverse occupations and businesses. Some were jewellers, some in the restaurant business, and others in tourism. He reached out and received them all. He did not believe that there should be any form of exclusivity that kept away a large section of the community that was less privileged. He recalls visiting temples and functions that Ambassadors in the past did not deign to attend.

Manju, a resident of Darjeeling, mentioned to me that she was on a visit to Bangkok sometime in 2015 when her money and documents were stolen. She missed her flight and was destitute, and it was a long weekend and the embassy was closed. She was desperate. As though in answer to her prayers, she recalled seeing a person in her hotel lobby who looked familiar. She walked up to him and inquired if he were from the embassy as she had seen him on Facebook. That person turned out to be Shringla. He not only lent her money from his personal account but ensured that she got an emergency passport to allow her to travel back home the same day. To this day, Manju remains awestruck at the kindness, generosity and spontaneity displayed by Shringla.

The other important task for Harsh Shringla in Thailand was to re-establish the cultural connection between India and Thailand, which was again something significant, and he worked extensively on it. He initiated the organisation of the first International Yoga Day in Thailand. Mr. Pradeep Agrawal, Chairman of Galaxy Group Companies, Thailand who sponsored the International Yoga Day in Thailand recalls that they were "expecting a couple of thousand people to participate in the programme but more than 7,000 people came to participate, even the Thai people appreciated it." The programme was a great success with more than expected active and enthusiastic participation from both the Indian and Thai communities. Shringla also initiated many cultural programmes like the *Festival of India* and *Father Bapu: Love for a Nation* to bring the diaspora community together and reconnect with the bhumi of their ancestors, to rekindle their feelings towards their homeland. These were also initiatives to reflect on the shared cultural ties between the two countries. He was greatly helped in this endeavour by his embassy colleagues, especially DCM G. Balasubramaniam and ICCR Director, Malathi Rao, among others.

In the words of Mr. Ramu Abbagani, who succeeded Balasubramaniam as DCM in the Embassy, Harsh Shringla is the "embodiment of Indian tradition and values" which is reflected in his efforts to organise the World Sanskrit Conference 2015 and Regional Hindi Conference 2014. Another significant programme was the *Thai-India Fun Fair* which was organised to establish a connection between Indian and Thai communities where people could interact and also generate awareness and interest among the Thai people about India and Indian culture and ethics. This was a significant tool of soft power to propagate India in Thailand. He paid attention to the extensive people-to-people contact which is one of the greatest contributions of Shringla—to connect people and to make people feel connected. In one such instance, he bought delegations of 31 people consisting of generals, admirals, secretaries, ministers, and the cream of Thai society to Darjeeling for the consecration of the remarkable Buddha statue that they paid for, which was made out of melted ammunition, as for "Thai people once an act of war now in use of peace is of the greatest merit." Shringla insisted that donations should be made to the poorest monasteries rather than to the monasteries that are rich and famous. The Thai donated statues of Buddha and his two disciples were installed at Dinchen Tashi Chholing Gumba at Singtam, Darjeeling. Shringla was able to nurture and harness the link between the people of Darjeeling and Thailand as many Thais who hold high posts have studied in Darjeeling and see Darjeeling as a beautiful place with a strong cultural heritage. Darjeeling is a go-to place for Thai students who want to learn English, and also because the people are very hospitable and friendly.

Harsh Shringla also knew how to change with time and how to adapt to new technology. He was well aware of the powers of social media, therefore with his officers he began the Facebook page of the Indian Embassy and the Embassy's Twitter account. This would make the Indian Embassy in Thailand more accessible and accountable, but most importantly it could connect to the common people. According to Mr. Samir Yamdagni, Executive Director, ITCC, "the use of technology in making the embassy a visible entity was recognised not only by the Indian diaspora but also by the Thai government which definitely contributed to improving the image of India."

Harsh Shringla served as the Indian Ambassador to Thailand for two years from January 2014 to January 2016. During his tenure, with regular political exchanges, and growing trade and investment, India's ties with Thailand evolved into a comprehensive partnership. The India-ASEAN FTA in Services and Investments was signed in September 2014 and came into force in July 2015. Prime Minister Narendra Modi and Prime Minister General Prayut Chan-o-cha held discussions on bilateral and regional issues of mutual interest on the sidelines of the India-ASEAN summit in Nay Pyi Taw on November 12, 2014. ASEAN-India connectivity is a shared strategic priority and India has made progress in implementing the India-Myanmar-Thailand Trilateral Highway and the Kaladan Multimodal Project.

External Affairs Minister Smt. Sushma Swaraj, visited Thailand to co-chair the 7th Meeting of the India-Thailand Joint Commission (JCM) and to attend the 16th World Sanskrit Conference in Bangkok from June 27 to 29, 2015. EAM called on Her Royal Highness Princess

Maha Chakri Sirindhorn and General Prem Tinsulanonda, President of the Privy Council of Thailand. EAM and Deputy Prime Minister and Minister of Foreign Affairs, General Tanasak Patimapragorn held delegation-level talks and discussed wide-ranging areas of economic and commercial cooperation, security, culture, science and technology, and information communication and technology, education, agriculture, legal and consular matters. Both Ministers exchanged the Instruments of Ratification of Extradition Treaty and signed the revised Double Taxation Avoidance Agreement, Memorandum of Understanding on the establishment of Nalanda University and witnessed the signing of MoU on establishing a Chair on Ayurveda at Rangsit University. The first meetings of the Joint Task Force (JTF) on Maritime Cooperation and Legal and Judicial Cooperation were held in New Delhi on October 27 and 28, 2015.

Another very successful visit was that of the newly appointed National Security Advisor, Shri Ajit Doval which resulted in extensive engagement on maritime security and other areas of strategic cooperation with Thailand. Shringla was actively engaged in the apprehension and extradition of terrorist Jagtar Singh Tara, wanted for the assassination of Punjab Chief Minister Beant Singh.

His contribution toward the Comprehensive Bilateral Economic and Commercial Partnership included the launch and promotion of the 'Make in India' Campaign in Thailand. Frequent buyer-seller meetings, business interaction and trade promotion events were organised keeping in mind that such initiative would further strengthen the economic ties between the two nations. This led to the formation of Indian Business Leaders Forum in Thailand. He recalls the very successful visit of the then Secretary of Industry, Mr. Amitabh Kanth to promote 'Make in India' and Thai investments in India along the Delhi-Mumbai Industrial Corridor.

Harsh Shringla redefined the Indian Embassy in Thailand by giving a new face, a new beginning, new hope and zeal to strive toward serving and connecting people. He has been exceedingly successful in regaining the confidence and trust of the Indians in Thailand; he initiated an effort to integrate the Thai community with Indians residing in Thailand. The Indo-Thai Trade Organisation considers him to be the "most beloved, fetching, revered, cherished ambassador to Thailand. They consider him to be the first ambassador to be so transparently available to the common man. He was always found standing amongst the common crowd and not to be separately seated high and above the rest. Inviting each and every individual seeker into his cabin and entertaining their problem at a personal level. Most grounded, and hence most loved!" Shringla gained the confidence and trust of the Indians residing in Thailand, assuring them that they will be heard.

8

DHAKA

(January 2016-December 2019)

IT IS often said, in diplomacy, that geography is destiny. A nation can choose its friends, but cannot choose its neighbours. This statement rings particularly true in respect of India and Bangladesh. India and Bangladesh share a land boundary that is more than 4,000 km long, one of the longest such boundaries in the world. Five Indian states, West Bengal, Assam, Meghalaya, Tripura and Mizoram, are contiguous to Bangladesh. The two countries share 54 rivers, the Sunderbans delta, and a common coastline on the Bay of Bengal.

Physical proximity is accompanied by a common history and a common heritage. Ethnic and religious ties are deep and enduring and linguistic and cultural ties run equally deep. Rabindranath Tagore has written the national anthems of both India and Bangladesh. Many commonly shared festivals are celebrated in both countries. Describing these linkages, Shringla while speaking to the Bangladesh Institute of International and Strategic Studies, during his visit to Dhaka as Foreign Secretary in March 2020, said: "We are joined by history, culture, and shared sacrifice just as much as we are joined by shared waters, the same cherished soil and fraternal ties. *Bangla maati* and *Baanglar jol* enrich and nurture both of us; they sustain our societies and they sustain our souls."

The recent history of relations between the two countries is packed with excitement. India played a key role in the Liberation of Bangladesh as an independent nation in the year 1971. Subsequently, there have been ups and downs, successes and disappointments between the two countries.

In January 2016, Harsh Shringla was appointed as India's High Commissioner to Bangladesh. The job of the High Commissioner of India in Dhaka is considered to be one of India's most sensitive and important diplomatic assignments. Shringla had been pulled out of Thailand before the completion of his tenure to be appointed Indian envoy to Bangladesh. This meant that he was professionally on the ascendant and was being tested to groom him as a future Foreign Secretary.

It was, however, difficult to find an officer better qualified than Harsh Shringla for this critical assignment. He had been Joint Secretary in the Ministry of External Affairs dealing with Bangladesh for several years. He had worked on many of the initiatives that had created the pathways for a transformed relationship with this neighbour. As High Commissioner, he would now work tirelessly to effect one of the most remarkable turnarounds in Indian diplomacy in its neighbourhood.

Former External Affairs Minister, the late Smt. Sushma Swaraj, while visiting Bangladesh in 2017 said that within the framework of Neighbourhood First, the fundamental spatial orientation of Indian foreign policy, it was "Bangladesh first". This was a remarkably clear statement of intent on the part of top Indian leadership and underscored the importance of the work that Shringla was, at that time, spearheading in Bangladesh. Speaking in a similar vein, Prime Minister Narendra Modi has described the current phase of India-Bangladesh relations as a "*sonali adhyaya*" or golden era.

High-level visits and summit meetings are the currency of diplomacy. They are events which require considerable preparation and effort. They represent the summation of activities and initiatives that are underway. The frequency and outcome of such visits is a "thermometer" that can capture the importance and the activity levels of the relationship. They also require careful choreography because of the symbolic meaning that they convey. By this yardstick, Shringla's tenure in Bangladesh coincided, not surprisingly, with an exceptionally large volume of traffic in high-level visits.

Prime Minister Sheikh Hasina visited India on five occasions during his tenure in Dhaka. She paid State visits to India twice, in April 2017, and in October 2019. She visited West Bengal twice in Shringla's tenure. In May 2018 she visited Shantiniketan for the inauguration of the Bangladesh Bhaban at Visva-Bharati University. Kazi Nazrul University, Asansol also conferred an honorary DLitt on the Prime Minister of Bangladesh. In November 2019, Prime Minister Sheikh Hasina and the Chief Minister of West Bengal, Mamata Banerjee jointly inaugurated the historic pink ball cricket test match between India and Bangladesh in Kolkata. She also visited Goa to attend the BRICS-BIMSTEC Outreach Summit in October 2016. The President of Bangladesh visited India in 2018.

The list of visitors from India during Shringla's tenure was also unprecedented. Defence Minister, the late Shri Manohar Parrikar visited Bangladesh in November 2016. In October 2017, the former External Affairs Minister, the late Smt. Sushma Swaraj visited Dhaka to attend the Joint Consultative Commission Meeting. Former Finance Minister, the late Shri Arun Jaitley, visited Bangladesh in October 2017. Home Minister Shri Rajnath Singh visited Bangladesh in July 2018.

It is extremely rare for the "big four" of the Union Council of Ministers, the Home Minister, the Defence Minister, the Finance Minister and the External Affairs Minister, to visit a country during the tenure of a Head of Mission. The only time that this happened in Bangladesh was during Harsh Shringla's tenure.

These visits contributed to the process by which the tone and the content of the relationship have been "reset". The website of the High Commission of India in Dhaka lists 27 items under its section on "Bilateral Mechanisms". An Observer Research Foundation publication states that, "Around 50 institutional mechanisms have been established between India and Bangladesh in areas of security, trade, power and energy, transport and connectivity, science and technology, defence, river management, and maritime affairs."

An overview of the reset India-Bangladesh relations—which coincided largely with Harsh Shringla's tenures as Joint Secretary dealing with Bangladesh and as High Commissioner in Dhaka—reveal a number of constituent megatrends. The first was the resolution of issues relating to the Land Boundary Agreement and the settlement relating to the maritime boundary. The second was the volume of development partnership projects underwritten in part by US$ 8 billion in Indian Lines of Credit. A third and related megatrend is the massive increase in connectivity between India and Bangladesh by road, railways, inland water and coastal shipping and by a combination of all of them. The fourth is the emergence of an economic space in which India is Bangladesh's second-largest trading partner, Bangladesh is India's largest trading partner in South Asia, increased investments, movement of people and the emergence of energy trading through interconnected grids and movement of hydrocarbons. The fifth and last is the understanding that India's North East and Bangladesh are organically linked and that this is where India's Act East and Neighbourhood First policies intersect. These development initiatives contributed immensely not only to the development of Bangladesh but also to the Northeastern states of India which share a border with Bangladesh enhancing deepening people-to-people linkages between the people of India and Bangladesh.

It is perhaps best to capture some of the movement in Shringla's own language. Speaking at an event organised by the Ananta Aspen Centre in 2021 as Foreign Secretary, he said that "India and Bangladesh are linked by rivers and share a coastline. Goods now reach Tripura from West Bengal through waterways via Ashuganj in Bangladesh or on coastal shipping via Chittagong port. Railways between countries are causing a 'rapid shrinking of South Asia's geography'. We have made a sustained effort with Bangladesh to leverage historical railway connections into a contemporary network. 5 of 6 rail links that linked Bangladesh and India, and were interrupted by the vagaries of history have been reactivated. Another rail link is being restored and a new rail link the Akhaura-Agartala railway, is being built. Railways have a lower carbon footprint than roadways and are usually more economical in moving large volumes of freight. The emerging railway networks are a win-win solution that can drive greater connectivity and growth in what we call BBIN—Bangladesh Bhutan India Nepal—configuration. They can, through Myanmar, provide a link to East and South East Asia. Passengers wishing to travel between India and Bangladesh can use trains such as Maitree and Bandhan Express or buses between Shillong and Dhaka and between Dhaka and Agartala and Kolkata. Kolkata is now linked to Agartala by bus via Dhaka."

In the same speech, he referred to the growing flow of energy between India and Bangladesh. He said "bulk LPG has been moving between India and Bangladesh since October 2019" and referred to the cross-border India-Bangladesh Friendship Pipeline linking Siliguri to Parbatipur that is being constructed. Power grids of India and Bangladesh are connected and "these connections allow India to currently supply about 1,160 MW of power to Bangladesh. India is also constructing the 1,320 MW Maitree Super Thermal Power Project in Bangladesh."

The groundwork for this transformation was laid in earlier years. The year 2017 was clearly a year in which there was transformational activity. The Ministry of External Affairs Annual Report for that period says that, "Prime Minister of Bangladesh, Sheikh Hasina, paid a State Visit to India in April 2017 following which tangible progress was made on mutually identified initiatives in multifaceted areas through broadening of cooperation and implementation of the decisions taken during the visit. At that time, the two sides had signed thirty-five bilateral and business agreements in areas such as space, nuclear energy, IT and electronics, development cooperation, defence, cybersecurity, trade and commerce, connectivity, power, capacity building, Media and Information."

Former External Affairs Minister, late Smt. Sushma Swaraj, followed by former Minister of Finance, late Shri Arun Jaitley Jaitely, visited Bangladesh that year. Agreements to extend the 3rd Line of Credit of US$ 4.5 billion expanding the total soft loan envelope to US$ 8 billion were concluded.

Bangladesh Finance Minister, Commerce Minister, Minister of Railways, Civil Aviation of Science and Technology, and State Minister of Youth and Sports, Biren Sikder paid official visits to take the bilateral agenda forward.

The Kolkata-Khulna-Dhaka bus service commenced operations in April 2017. The Bandhan Express between Kolkata and Khulna and end-to-end immigration and customs services for the existing Maitree Express (between Kolkata and Dhaka) at the International Rail Passenger Terminus at Kolkata were inaugurated in November 2017.

2018, the second year of Shringla's tenure in Dhaka, was equally momentous. The Ministry of External Affairs reports for that period attest to the continuing momentum. It says that, "In the past four years, the imperative of expanding bilateral ties has taken on an all-of-Government character, with departments ranging from Power, Defence and Commerce to Ministries of I&B, Shipping, P&NG all developing new programmes for bilateral cooperation. In pursuit of this perspective, Governments of both sides have expedited work to ensure the utilisation of India's three credit lines—which total almost US$ 8 billion; the highest allocation on credit lines as well as the best terms India has offered so far. Bangladesh is also a major recipient of grant aid, with thirty-five Small Development Projects completed, and a further forty in progress."

Moreover "in September 2018, construction works of the following projects in Bangladesh under Government of India Lines of Credit/grant financing were inaugurated: (i) 500 MW additional power supply from India to Bangladesh; (ii) Akhaura-Agartala rail link; (iii) rehabilitation of the Kulaura-Shahbazpur section of Bangladesh Railways; (iv) a 130 km India-Bangladesh Friendship Pipeline from Siliguri to Parbatipur, Bangladesh, and (v) additional rail lines of Dhaka-Tongi-Joydevpur section of Bangladesh Railway." Two more significant items are included, first, "In solidarity with Bangladesh's efforts to provide succour to those displaced from North Rakhine State in Myanmar, India launched Operation Insaniyat and supplied three tranches of humanitarian aid." The second says that, in "July 2018, Home Affairs Minister Shri Rajnath Singh visited Bangladesh, and discussed ways to strengthen the anti-terror mechanism between New Delhi and Dhaka."

His first year as High Commissioner, 2016, was equally eventful. In June 2016, Bangladesh allowed Indian goods to transit to the North East via Bangladesh. The fourth railway line between the two countries through Radhikapur-Birol was made ready. The Petrapole Integrated Check Post (ICP) to facilitate the cross-border movement of people and goods and the Phulbari-Banglabandha immigration check-post were inaugurated. 2016 also saw a significant amendment to the Extradition Treaty during the visit of the Home Minister of Bangladesh.

The then Defence Minister, Shri Manohar Parrikar visited Bangladesh in November-December 2016. It was the first visit by an Indian Defence Minister since 1971. It was a visit that significantly altered the nature of the interaction between the Indian and Bangladeshi defence establishments. It deepened security ties and set the stage for numerous agreements that were finalised in time for Sheikh Hasina's visit to India within a few months of Shri Parrikar's visit. These were an MoU between Defence Service Staff College, Wellington and Defence Services Command and Staff College, Mirpur, for Enhancing Cooperation Concerning Military Education in the Field of Strategic and Operational Studies; an MoU between the National Defence Colleges of India and Bangladesh for Enhancing Cooperation in the Field of National Security, Development and Strategic Studies. An MoU between India and Bangladesh on Cooperation in the Peaceful Uses of Outer Space. During his visit, Shri Parrikar also discussed naval cooperation including coordinated patrolling along the International Maritime Boundary Line (IMBL), bilateral maritime exercises, joint surveillance of the Exclusive Economic Zone and cooperation in hydrography.

The first inaugural Coordinated Patrol (CORPAT) between the navies of India and Bangladesh was conducted on June 27-July 4, 2018 during Shringla's tenure. This was the first time a coordinated patrol was organised between the two nations.

This was Shringla at his best. Years of working on this relationship and decades of experience in government meant that he was able to consolidate the progress that was taking place along multiple axes of bilateral relations. Whether it was political relations, economic ties, development partnerships, connectivity or people-to-people contacts, he demonstrated an ability to "get things done". He also showed, once again, an ability to navigate a politically sensitive atmosphere in which a capacity to take everyone along was essential. A non-confrontational and constructive attitude meant that he was able to detect and defuse potential problems and get the Indian and Bangladeshi systems to operate in harmony.

He travelled tirelessly, exploring and understanding the culture and traditions of Bangladeshi people, who were always accessible to laymen. The record of his years in Bangladesh is that of diplomacy at its most active and most effective.

Not all his achievements were related to the bilateral sphere. He was able to play an important role in dampening the tensions that could potentially arise due to the Rohingya problem between Myanmar and Bangladesh. It had a spill-over effect on the regional equation and on broader questions of international law and politics. Here, again, Mr. Shringla's vast experience and diplomatic acumen helped. He coordinated India's aid to the Rohingya camps, delivered in several tranches through Operation Insaniyat, and navigated tensions on the issue between Bangladesh and Myanmar, both important neighbours for India.

He also worked tirelessly on promoting linkages between Bangladesh and the states of North-East India. He visited the North-Eastern states and also arranged visits by Shri Gautam Deb, West Bengal Minister of Tourism & North Bengal Affairs, and present Assam Chief Minister and then Assam Finance Minister, Shri Himanta Biswa Sarma, PWD Minister, Shri Parimal Suklabaidya, to Bangladesh.

Harsh Shringla's tenure did have its difficult and dark moments. Among the tasks that fell to him was to handle the fallout of the terrorist attack at the Holey Artisan Bakery in Dhaka in July 2016. Shringla was in Delhi at the time that the terrorists took diners (mainly foreigners) at an upmarket cafe in Dhaka hostage. One of the hostages was a young Indian girl, Tarishi, studying in Berkeley, California, in Dhaka on vacation to meet her parents. As advised by the then Foreign Secretary Dr. S. Jaishankar, Shringla rushed back to Dhaka only to find that the terrorists had heinously murdered all their hostages, including Tarishi. Shringla described this as one of the worst moments of his life when he had to meet and console the parents of Tarishi and accompany them with all the other bereaved families to the Military Hospital in Dhaka where the bodies were laid out on the verandah for the families to identify.

Shringla realised early on in his tenure in Dhaka that while the two countries enjoyed a close relationship at the Governmental level, the same did not appear true at the level of the common man. The average Bangladeshi having been fed anti-India rhetoric over decades was hard-wired to blame many of the country's ills on India's actions. What was needed was reassuring actions and the removal of irritants where possible. One area of long-standing neglect was the visa regime that India applied to Bangladesh. While no visa fees were levied out of consideration for a close relationship, it was evident that securing an Indian visa was an arduous task.

At the time Shringla came to Bangladesh in 2016, the Indian High Commission issued some 5 lakh visas a year. This was based on an online appointment system which was oversubscribed within a few minutes of its opening every morning. Clearly, the demand far exceeded the supply but no one knew by how much. Shringla recalls having to drive to the office every morning past a snaking line of visa applicants that waited for hours under the scorching sun without any guarantee to make it to the end of the line. He believes he could feel the resentment oozing out of them every time his car with the Indian flag went past. He was empathetic to their plight and, at the same time, he understood that fixing the visa system would remove one of the main irritants in the Bangladeshi public's mind directed towards India.

Before he left, Shringla made sure he had the backing of his own authorities in his endeavour. The then External Affairs Minister, Sushma Swaraj and Foreign Secretary, Dr. Jaishankar were both aware of the resentment caused by the inadequacies of the visa system and wanted it resolved on priority. Smt. Swaraj told Shringla to do whatever it took to sort out the visa problem. Shringla assured her that this would be resolved before she visited Bangladesh. On his part, Dr. Jaishankar made sure the system was fully supportive in backing. Shringla is on this mission. He assigned Shringla's close friend and batchmate, Mukta Tomar, who was then Additional Secretary in the Ministry, the task of coordinating actions in Delhi. It took Mukta Tomar as many as ten meetings convened in Delhi with Shringla present to provide support from headquarters to strengthen the visa system.

Harsh Shringla took a personal interest in relaxing outdated visa restrictions on Bangladeshis visiting India and in improving visa operations in his High Commission. He focused on improving the experience for Bangladeshis applying for Indian visas, introducing innovations such as granting longer-term visas, enhancing backroom processing capacity and opening a Visa Application Centre at the centre of Dhaka that could comfortably seat 700 applicants. His objective was to ensure that the experience of securing an Indian visa became as smooth as possible. As a result of his efforts, the issuance of Indian visas for Bangladeshi nationals increased from 5 lakh to 15 lakh per annum. More than a million Bangladeshis visit India annually. It was calculated that these visitors spend as much as US$ 4 billion a year in India. The money that they spend has a considerable impact on the economies of neighbouring states like West Bengal and Sikkim which have benefited directly from high-income Bangladeshi tourists who visit India for shopping, entertainment and medical purposes. All this was made possible due to the reforms in visa policy undertaken single-mindedly by Shringla.

Smt. Sushma Swaraj and Dr. Jaishankar did visit Bangladesh to inaugurate the new High Commission building in August 2017. True to his word, Shringla had not only resolved the constraints in the visa system, he had also identified 15 quick impact community development projects for Smt. Sushma Swaraj to announce. Shringla told the audience present at the high-level event that within a year of the Minister's laying the foundation stones, all 15 projects would be completed to satisfaction. As it happened, by the end of 2018, 14 of the 15 projects were completed. Only one, the Ramna Kali Bari renovation project, remained stalled due to an internal conflict within the managing committee of the temple. So it was of some satisfaction to Shringla that three years later he accompanied the President of India to inaugurate the now-completed temple project. He had come full circle.

To connect India and Bangladesh through education, around 50 leading educational institutes and universities from India participated in the 5th India Education Fair (July 18-19, 2018) that was held in Dhaka by SAPE Events & Media. Monitoring elections and electoral results are one of the key challenges faced by Indian heads of mission in neighbouring countries with democratic traditions. Electoral outcomes are difficult to predict and often have foreign policy consequences. Shringla ended his tenure in Dhaka soon after the general elections in Bangladesh in 2018. Sheikh Hasina and the Awami League were re-elected to power. It was, in many ways, a fitting end for a successful stint as Indian envoy to Bangladesh. The work that had been done on building bilateral relations with one of India's most important diplomatic partners would continue with established partners. His legacy would be in hands that would be willing to take it forward.

9

WASHINGTON

(January 2019-January 2020)

THE RELATIONSHIP between India and the United States is the most significant diplomatic account that India has, and has been described as one of the most important diplomatic relationships in the 21st century. The website of the Ministry of External Affairs states that "India-U.S. bilateral relations have developed into a 'global strategic partnership', based on shared democratic values and increasing convergence of interests on bilateral, regional and global issues." This depicts the importance of strategic partnership with the United States.

The United States also sees India as one of its most important partners. According to the US State Departments Fact Sheet on "US Relations with

India", "The United States supports India's emergence as a leading global power and vital partner in efforts to ensure that the Indo-Pacific is a region of peace, stability, and growing prosperity." A summit-level joint issued in June 2016 called the India-US relationship an "Enduring Global Partners in the 21st Century".

Harsh Shringla was sent to Washington in January 2019, after his tenure in Dhaka. With his appointment as Ambassador of India to the United States he set foot on to the very top of the diplomatic profession. He was India's representative to the most powerful nation in the world, as almost all nations consider the United States to be their most important partner. Their Ambassadors in Washington are usually their ablest or most influential diplomats. Mr. Shringla's appointment to this position was not just a great honour, it was indeed a recognition of his abilities and his skill established after more than 34 years of hard work and dedicated service.

Shringla's appointment as Ambassador to the USA was a huge leg-up and a mark of confidence reposed in him by the Prime Minister and the establishment. In many senses, this represented the pinnacle of his diplomatic career. Given the stalwarts that had occupied the office, he had reason to be both anxious and eager at the start of his ambassadorial stint in the US.

Shringla, it is to be noted, became Ambassador to the United States at the age of 55 years. This made him the youngest Indian to hold that position. This was not, however, a position in which he could rest on his laurels. Much was at stake. To begin with, the Ambassador coordinated a vast and complicated diplomatic machinery that kept the wheels of the India-US relationship running. The US State Department's view about this machinery states that "there are more than thirty bilateral dialogues and working groups, which span all aspects of human endeavour, from space and health cooperation to energy and high technology trade. These include the US-India Counterterrorism Joint Working Group, which was established in 2000 and is among our oldest government-to-government dialogues, as well as the Strategic Energy Partnership, Cyber Dialogue, Civil Space Working Group, Trade Policy Forum, Defense Policy Group and many more."

The Government of India states that "there are more than 50 bilateral dialogue mechanisms between the two governments." These dialogue mechanisms have their apex in Summit-level meetings and in the 2+2 meetings, which both took place during Shringla's eventful tenure in the United States. Prime Minister Modi visited the United States in September 2019 where he met President Donald Trump and also addressed the historic "Howdy Modi" rally. Shringla planned and organised the "Howdy Modi" event that saw US President Donald Trump and Prime Minister Narendra Modi address a rally together, and strengthened India-US defence ties considerably during his short tenure. In December 2019, the United States hosted the second 2+2 Ministerial Dialogue in Washington. External Affairs Minister Dr. S. Jaishankar and Defence Minister Rajnath Singh met the US Secretaries of State and Defense. President Trump and Prime Minister also interacted in multilateral events during the G7 meeting in Biarritz, which led to deepening bilateral ties between the oldest and largest democratic countries in the world.

2019 was a year in which Prime Minister Modi secured a resounding victory for a second term in office. Shringla saw the outcome of elections as key to taking India's comprehensive global strategic partnership with the United States to the next level. In an effort to ensure that he saw through the elections in critical neighbouring Bangladesh before demitting office there, he had travelled directly from Dhaka to DC. As he recalls, he was transported from tropical Bangladesh to DC's frigid Beltway in a matter of days. He remembers being bewildered at the pace of change. On January 6, Shringla took leave from Prime Minister Sheikh Hasina at Ganabhaban and on January 11, barely two days after his arrival in Washington, D.C., he was presenting his credentials to President Trump at the White House Oval Office. In other words, he hit the ground running.

A press release on the credentials ceremony said that "President Trump warmly welcomed Ambassador Shringla to Washington and wished him every success in his high responsibilities as India's Ambassador to the United States. The President fondly recalled his friendship with Prime Minister Modi and his recent telephone conversation with the Prime Minister. He highlighted the broad range of strategic interests and fundamental democratic values shared between the two countries."

Shringla, in his remarks, conveyed warm greetings from the President and the Prime Minister of India to President Trump and the First Lady; he added further that India was greatly encouraged by the President's strong personal commitment to take the India-US strategic partnership forward and assured President Trump of his commitment to "expand key pillars of the bilateral relationship including economic relations and trade ties, defence and security, energy, science and technology and global issues, among others."

India's economic and commercial relationship with the United States is substantial. The United States is one of India's largest trading partners. Exports and imports of goods and services amounted to US$ 142 billion in 2018. Trade between the two countries has been growing at a compounded annual rate of more than 10% annually. It is also a relationship where there are major flows of Foreign Direct Investment. Some of the largest foreign investments in India have been from the United States. The largest and best-known US companies, Amazon, Facebook, Google, Walmart all made huge investments in India in the recent past. These include US$ 15 billion by Walmart, US$ 10 billion from Google and US$ 5 billion from Facebook. This high-profile, high-volume investments and rapidly growing trade meant that Shringla was also on one of the most important seats for Indian economic diplomacy.

Shringla's economic diplomacy was multifaceted. He established contact with major US businessmen in significant sectors. India is one of the major centres of gravity in the global energy scenario. He exploited the potential of the Indian energy market adroitly to focus US attention on the size and vitality of the Indian economy as well as on its growth potential. He pointed out that India purchased more than US$ 4.5 billion of oil and gas from the United States.

This adroitness was necessary in light of Shringla's arrival in Washington at a time when President Trump and his team introduced major modifications—and, some would say, disruptions—in American trade policies. The US-China trade war, with its reassessment of long-standing trade practices and imposition of sanctions and other measures, changed the nature of the playing field in which diplomats like Shringla operated. Major challenges included the announcement, in March 2019, by US trade representative Robert Lighthizer, that the US would terminate India's designation as a beneficiary developing country under the Generalised System of Preferences (GSP) programme. It was a time when some strong statements about Indian trade policies were made by the highest levels of the US government. This was also a time when American IT majors and e-commerce giants were trying to establish themselves in India and were raising issues such as data localisation that impacted them. Shringla had to find a way to keep the attention focused on the positive elements of the India-US economic relationship and its huge potential upside while sensitising US policymakers about the imperatives that guided Indian economic decision-making. He facilitated a large number of discussions with US authorities, particularly the US Trade Representative and the Department of Commerce. The discussions were led by Commerce Minister Piyush Goyal from the Indian side which, to some extent, helped in bridging the gap. Effective communication and diplomacy were the keys for Shringla.

Speaking at a farewell reception on January 8, 2020, in Washington, D.C., just before his departure, he said that, "what we are really looking for is to provide the basis for an exclusive partnership in trade between our two countries that can give US companies preferential market access to India and Indian companies preferential market access to the United States."

When interacting with the broader business and economic audience, he followed a simple but high-impact strategy. He drew attention to areas in which the Indian market was creating massive selling opportunities for the US industry. Amidst intense negotiations between India and the US to resolve their trade differences, Shringla emphasised the bilateral trade between India and America which has the potential to double and reach US$280 billion in the next five years. He described the trade differences as minor speed bumps that come along the way, and innovative policy measures could assist in greater involvement of US companies in India and vice versa. He drew attention to three sectors that could have a transformational effect on bilateral trade and investment and these were civil aviation, defence and energy. He also spotlighted another area about which not much was known—the volume of Indian investment in the United States.

In remarks to Senate India Caucus and Congressional Caucus on India and Indian-Americans, Shringla said that, "in 2008, the US has bagged more than $18 billion in arms contracts with India including the C-17 Globemaster and C-130J transport planes, P-8 (I) maritime reconnaissance aircraft, M777 light-weight howitzer, Harpoon missiles and Apache and Chinook helicopters. We have started the import of US crude and natural gas worth $4.5 billion every year. Our private airlines have placed orders for around 300 Boeing aircraft to be delivered over the next 5 to 7 years that are worth around $39 billion and will create 130,000 American jobs."

A visit by Finance Minister Nirmala Sitharaman and other top businessmen was leveraged to highlight India's potential as a market and a source of investments. India's status as a Major Defence Partner and deepened cooperation on maritime security, interoperability, and information sharing were highlighted by Shringla in his interactions and he worked hard to expand these ties. He took a personal interest in expanding defence ties. Apache and Chinook helicopters were inducted into Indian Air Force during his tenure with Shringla himself taking delivery of the first Chinooks at the Boeing Defense facility in Philadelphia on January 31, 2019. He used the opportunity to focus attention on the growing industry partnerships between Indian and US companies such as Boeing. This was important both in the bilateral context and in the context of the effort to 'Make in India'.

Shringla was accessible to businessmen. The social media pages of the Embassy of India and Washington during this time show numerous meetings with both American and Indian captains of industry. These include meetings with high-profile CEOs such as Sundar Pichai of Google. He worked particularly closely and interacted frequently with the major chambers of commerce and industry in Washington that were focused on promoting business ties between the two countries led by Ambassador Nisha Biswal, former US Assistant Secretary of State, who headed the US India Business Council (USIBC) and Dr. Mukesh Aghi, who headed the US-India Strategic Partnership Forum (USISPF).

The high-level access that he had to the world of business became apparent during the Round Table meeting of the CEOs of the world's largest energy companies during the Prime Minister's visit to the United States in September 2019. He mobilised a virtual who's who of the global energy industry to meet the Prime Minister. These included top executives from Air Products, Baker Hughes, BP PLC, Cheniere Energy, Dominion Energy, Emerson Electric Company, ExxonMobil, Perot Group and Hillwood, IHS Markit, LyondellBasell Industries, McDermott, Schlumberger, Tellurian Inc., Total S.A., Vinmar International and Westlake Chemicals. Resulting in great success, bilateral trade reached its highest point ever, and two-way investments saw substantial increases during this period.

Prime Minister Modi won a historic victory in the general elections in May 2019. The elections were closely followed by the US leadership. Within hours of the announcement of the results, President Trump tweeted, "Congratulations to Prime Minister @NarendraModi and his BJP party on their BIG election victory! Great things are in store for the US-India partnership with the return of PM Modi at the helm." It was obvious that Shringla would be at the centre of a major exercise to impart further momentum to the work underway in sectors such as defence, trade and investments.

A unique feature of the India-US bilateral relationship is the diaspora. According to the US Department of State: "The strong people-to-people ties between our countries, reflected in a four million-strong Indian American diaspora, are a tremendous source of strength for the partnership." Shringla succeeded in connecting with the diaspora as few other Indian Ambassadors had. With his informality and down-to-earth nature, he connected easily with Indians and Indian Americans across the country. He developed an excellent rapport with the community and his list of contacts spanned the humblest Indians to the tallest representatives of this extremely successful and dynamic community. Shringla opened his home, in Washington's prestigious Macomb Street locality, to leaders and members of the community, and hosted several meetings and receptions for them.

The traditional Republic Day and Independence Day events organised by the Embassy were turned into national events with guests coming to Washington from different parts of the country. Special attention was given to regional festivals. Baisakhi, for example, was celebrated with gusto in May 2019, it was attended by over 200 guests, including prominent representatives of Sikh organisations and Gurudwaras from the Washington area, San Francisco, New York and Delaware, prominent community leaders, and media. Other festivals such as Diwali were also celebrated with equal enthusiasm and wide participation.

The high point of 2019 was the visit of Prime Minister Modi to the USA in September 2019. This saw an extraordinarily unique event in the annals of relations between states in the form of "Howdy Modi" on September 22, 2019. This was the first time ever that a Prime Minister of India had addressed a record gathering of 50,000 US citizens of Indian origin, along with the President of the United States. The event had a bipartisan character and was attended by a number of Senators and Congressmen.

Howdy Modi was one of the most impressive displays of Shringla's leadership skills and organisational abilities. Around 45,000 Indians and Indian Americans attended this once-in-a-lifetime event that was addressed jointly by Prime Minister Modi and President Donald Trump. It was possibly the largest gathering attended by a visiting head of government in the United States. It was also one of the largest public meetings in recent times in the United States. Shringla and his team of Consuls General across the country worked closely with the Texas India Forum (TIF) to organise the event. The venue, Houston's NRG stadium, was selected after a lot of deliberation. He made a low-key trip to Houston to give direction to initial efforts. Thereafter, separate groups—each headed by a Consul General—were constituted, to manage individual aspects of the function. They worked closely and organically with the hundreds of volunteers of the Texas India Forum on various components of the programme and its complex logistics. He instituted a system of daily video conferences and milestones that led up to the programme.

The Texas India Forum created an electronic platform to manage the invitations and access for the event. This required to be coordinated with the databases of Indian diaspora associations and those of the Embassy in Washington and the Consulates in various parts of the United States. Although the bulk of the participants came from Houston and Dallas—which have some of the largest concentrations of Indian populations in the country—a special effort was made to mobilise attendance from across the country. It soon became apparent that the attendance would be larger than expected. Initial projections were that about 25,000 people would attend. This required a midstream course correction by the organisers and by Shringla's team. All aspects of the event including stadium arrangements, security and the flow of events had to be modified to accommodate this interest. No detail was forgotten, simultaneous interpretation, for example, was organised not just in English but also in Spanish.

Media interest in the programme was enormous. A massive media contingent from India travelled to Houston to cover the event. It was broadcast live to an audience that was estimated to be in the hundreds of millions.

The event was initially to be addressed by Prime Minister Modi. However, as plans picked up momentum, the possibility of President Trump attending the event emerged. This had to be kept a secret and plans were made, with the top organisers, in the utmost confidence to accommodate President Trump in the programme. This required a sensitive coordination with the White House and the organisers. Eventually, a programme was carefully crafted. Given the relative paucity of precedents, Mr. Shringla had to personally work on several complicated questions that related to reconciling protocol and security requirements with the flow of events of a function of this nature. The Prime Minister's programme and that of the President of the United States were synchronised to the finest detail. Security, with the tens of thousands of spectators in a stadium, had to be supervised with the greatest care and required a major effort by Shringla's team, the US Secret Service, the city of Houston authorities, the Special Protection Group and Indian law enforcement agencies.

The Texas India Forum that organised this event created an electronic platform to manage the invitations and access for the event. Shringla took this rare challenge head-on and was actively involved. This required coordination with the databases of Indian diaspora associations. He geared his own colleagues in the Embassy and Consulate with those of the Embassy in Washington and the Consulates in various parts of the United States to impart highest degree of team spirit. As preparations picked up momentum, the possibility of President Trump attending the event emerged. This required rigorous coordination with the federal, state and city authorities in the United States besides the White House to assist the Texas India Forum to make secure that the various aspects of this event such as security, protocol and logistical issues were meticulously addressed. Media interest in the programme was enormous. Shringla recalls the pre-event coordination dinner hosted by Dr. Anupam Ray at his residence for the entire White House advance team in Houston.

According to media reports, some anti-Indian groups made elaborate plans to embarrass Prime Minister Modi. They went so far as to seek permission from the city authorities to demonstrate inside the stadium. Shringla's team made a special effort to liaise with local authorities led by Houston Mayor Sylvester Turner and Police Chief Art Acevado on these and other issues. The city of Houston, which had not seen an event of this nature and magnitude, cooperated in full measure.

Shringla personally monitored and supervised each of the many moving parts that made this rally a memorable one. It was the largest gathering for a foreign leader in the United States and one of the largest gatherings ever addressed by President Trump in the United States. All this was achieved within a period of less than three months.

A round table meeting of the CEOs of the world's largest energy companies was organised during the Prime Minister's visit to the United States in September 2019. A virtual who's who of the global energy industry met the Prime Minister. These included top executives from Air Products, Baker Hughes, BP PLC, Cheniere Energy, Dominion Energy, Emerson Electric Company, ExxonMobil, Perot Group and Hillwood, IHS Markit, LyondellBasell Industries, McDermott, Schlumberger, Tellurian Inc., Total S.A., Vinmar International and Westlake Chemicals.

Almost as important as the outreach was the fact that Mr. Shringla took enormous care to seek bipartisan support for good relations with India. He had equally good relations with such Democratic luminaries as House Speaker Nancy Pelosi of California as he had with prominent Republican Senators such as John Cornyn of Texas. The social media pages of the Embassy and the Consulates during his tenure are replete with posts about his meeting Senators and Congressmen across the political spectrum as he gave particular attention to meeting Committee Chairs and legislative leaders in key positions.

Shringla was fortunate in that India was highly regarded by Republicans and Democrats alike. In the immediate aftermath of the terrorist attack at Pulwama in Jammu and Kashmir in February 2019, it was not only President Trump and senior members of the Administration that tweeted and made statements condemning Pakistan for its acts of terrorism, but over 60 prominent individuals across the political spectrum in the US that came out strongly in solidarity with India.

The Government's decision to abrogate Article 370 and impose temporary restrictions in the UT of Jammu and Kashmir evoked sharp reactions from an unusual alliance of liberals and Islamic radicals alike—and Pakistan actively—and openly stoked the fires. A major challenge arose in the form of a one-sided and factually unjustified draft resolution floated by an Indian-origin Congresswoman Pramila Jayapal in her quest to garner the support of the left fringe of the Democratic Party.

Shringla and his team carried out an intense campaign at Capitol Hill to articulate the factually correct position and to highlight the damage such a resolution could do to the relationship. He met a record 400 Senators and Congressmen and travelled to 22 US states meeting Governors, State Senators and key influencers. This helped greatly when it came to placing in perspective steps taken by the Government of India to abrogate Article 370 of the Constitution and to adopt the Constitutional Amendment Act (CAA).

Shringla received an assurance from the Administration that they would be loath to support such a biased resolution. The India Caucuses in the Senate and House stood solidly behind this position. The Republicans, with one exception, refused to support this document. In fact, Congressman after Congressman took the floor of the house to applaud Prime Minister Modi and his policies for development as well as the strong steps taken by him to strengthen India-US relations. Some Congressmen who made notable interventions in support of India in their statements at the Hill were Scott Perry; Francis Rooney; Joe Wilson; Pete Olson; Paul Gosar; and George Holding.

Appearing on Fox News, CNN and MSNBC in prime time, Shringla used the media extensively to articulate his Government's position on the clear benefits of the abrogation of Article 370 for the people of Jammu and Kashmir and Ladakh. He highlighted the steps the Government had taken to fast-track development and bring investment into the state. He clarified that restrictions such as the closure of the internet and curfew were also being rapidly addressed.

Before finishing his term of office in DC, Shringla explained the serious reservations he had on tabling the controversial draft at the Foreign Affairs Committee of the House to its Chair, Congressman Eliot Engel. As a result of his eloquent argument, Engel was convinced and a decision was taken to postpone tabling of the resolution until after the Christmas and winter recess of the House. By the time the House convened in 2020, developments on the ground, including the normalisation of life in Jammu and Kashmir and a visit by Ambassadors based in New Delhi—including the US Ambassador—to Jammu and Kashmir, overtook matters. The resolution never saw the light of day.

The year was not without its challenges. Shringla recalls that soon after he took over, a separatist outfit, the Sikhs For Justice, (SFJ) made a public announcement that it would burn the Indian national flag in front of the Indian Embassy in Washington, D.C. on Republic Day. Having sought recourse from the US system and failed to get any assurances due to apparent legal impediments, Shringla was at a loss. Yet, he found it hard to accept this blatant challenge to national pride, and decided that he had no option but to engage directly to prevent this anti-national act that the SFJ intended to use to publicly humiliate the Indian state. Taking all of his colleagues into confidence, hundreds of students and Embassy family members converged at the Mahatma Gandhi Park outside the Embassy and resorted to Gandhiji's time-tested policy of non-violence to prevent SFJ activists from attempting to denigrate Indian sentiment. As a result of a day-long vigil in sub-zero temperatures by courageous students, women and children, the SFJ activists were kept at a distance from the Embassy and had to finally concede defeat by returning home without fulfilling their publicly stated goal. This was a victory of the power of the people over misguided radical sentiment. It was also a setback for the SFJ, one which its founder acknowledged as much on Twitter, albeit with much vitriol. Later, this policy was replicated by Indian Consulates across the United States, successfully keeping demonstrators against Article 370 abrogation or CAA at bay. Some insiders opined that had the Indian High Commission in London followed a similar bold policy, the vandalism of its premises would have been prevented. Leadership and courage in the performance of public duties do matter.

The Indian Ambassador to the United States supervises the largest team in the Indian diplomatic establishment. The Embassy in Washington is one of the biggest with independent Political, Economic, Commercial, Consular, Press, Information and Cultural, Space, Military, Naval, Air Force, Community Affairs, Personnel, Administration, Space and Defence Technology Wings. In addition, Shringla supervised the Consulates General of India in New York, San Francisco, Houston, Chicago and Atlanta. The Consulates in New York and San Francisco are larger than many Embassies.

The Ambassador of India in Washington also oversees a large public service delivery organisation through its consular operations. These can be challenging at times. Soon after Shringla took over as Ambassador in Washington, he faced an unprecedented situation with a US immigration crackdown on Indian students about the misuse of their visa status. About 600 Indian students were detained and sentenced by US immigration authorities. In an undercover "sting" operation, US law enforcement officials enticed Indian students to register at a "Farmington University" that was being run by undercover US agents. Dozens of Indian students fell for this ruse which promised visas for students enrolled in a course that had no classes. He made sure that Indian officials travelled to each part of the US where Indian students are based to provide consular access, guidance and legal assistance wherever required. Working closely with community associations and the education sector, the issue was resolved successfully.

However, Shringla clearly indicated that a sting operation after setting up a fake university to lure students to seek admission would not have happened in India and further pointed out the difference between Indian law and American law. In Indian law, "we don't have this concept of entrapment. We only investigate when there is a sense of guilt, when there is a sense of someone has committed an act that is a criminal act or misdemeanour. That act is investigated and then you come out with evidence. But you don't intentionally lure people into a situation where they make mistakes and commit criminal acts or acts that can be in contradiction with the law of the land you live in."

The United States is a federal polity. Washington, though the capital, is only one of the great cities of the United States. Shringla felt that in order to understand a federal state like the US and to comprehensively engage, he needed to travel and connect widely across the country. In the span of a year in office, he visited a record 22 of the 50 US states and travelled tirelessly during his short tenure across the country to meet important interlocutors and to connect with India-related interests. India has Consulates General in New York, San Francisco, Chicago, Houston and Atlanta. Each covered several states with major concentrations of US companies doing business in India, Indian businesses investing in the United States as well as other institutions with interests in India. Some US states like California, Texas, Florida and New York had economies that were larger than that of most countries. The GDP of Texas was larger than that of Russia. The city of Houston housed not only the oil and gas companies that were interested in India and several hundred thousand Indians but also had the US headquarters of Oil India Ltd., ONGC Videsh, and had a major presence of Reliance Industries, the Adani Group, L&T, Mahindra, TCS, Wipro and Infosys. One of his major contributions was to make local leaders across the United States aware of the Indian presence and Indian investments in their areas. This in turn generated interest in trade missions by US states in various cities in India.

Shringla took the opportunity to address the universities wherever he travelled, from Harvard (School of Government) and Stanford (Business School) to the University of North Carolina at Chapel Hill, and George Washington University in Washington, D.C. His visits were always gruelling but that did not dissuade him from engaging with young minds. On one of his visits to Boston, Massachusetts in December 2019, he met the Governor of Massachusetts, Charlie Baker IV, Mohan Nannapaneni, Founder of Team Aid, an organisation working for the welfare of the Indian diaspora in the US, and delivered a keynote address on "The next phase of India's growth and Development" at the Harvard Kennedy School. He interacted enthusiastically with researchers and students of the Harvard India Caucus and other universities, and at the same time addressed and interacted with members of the New England Council, the oldest regional council in the USA, and addressed prominent representatives of the Indian community at a reception hosted by the India Association of Greater Boston.

On another visit to Kentucky in May 2019 he met Governor Matt Bevin and had an extensive business engagement with UPS Worldport, GE Appliances, Beam Suntory, etc. He also attended a USIBC business round table event with Kentucky business leaders, including the President and CEO of the Kentucky Chamber of Commerce, interacted with the Directors of the Western Kentucky University and the University of Louisville and Indian students in Kentucky, and visited the Shri Maninagar Swaminarayan Temple—which had witnessed an incident of vandalism in January 2019—to deliver a message of solidarity to the Indian community.

He gave particular attention to the largest American states—California and Texas—met and interacted extensively with the Governor of California Gavin Newsom, the Governor of Texas Greg Abbott, and the Mayors of Houston, Dallas and Los Angeles. In Texas, he reached out to representatives of top business enterprises, diaspora associations, educational institutions and healthcare entities. He also used his visit to Texas to focus attention on another rapidly emerging dimension of Indian investments in the United States by convening a meeting of Indian businesses headquartered in Texas. One of his memorable meetings in Texas was with former President George W. Bush and Mrs. Laura Bush in Dallas.

Another memorable trip was to Alaska where he visited Anchorage and Fairbanks, at the invitation of US Senator Dan Sullivan, mainly to visit the US military bases where joint "Red Flag" exercises are conducted. He also visited Arkansas which has substantial Indian investments such as Welspun and TCS, and US companies such as Walmart and Tyson Foods with major investments in India, and attended a Colorado India Business Round Table. Shringla's visits were key to convincing the Governors of Colorado and Arkansas, Jared Polis and Asa Hutchison, and several other

Governors of American states to visit India with trade delegations so that they could access the true essence of India and its economic potential.

Shringla was struck by the incredible receptivity to India in the United States. The unlimited access he had to the White House where he had the opportunity to call on President Trump on three different occasions, White House Chiefs of Staff, Senators and Congressmen, top CEOs—including a memorable dinner with Google CEO Sundar Pichai—the military leadership, media, academia and think tanks. The greatest support came from the US Administration, in particular, the Department of State.

Public diplomacy and promoting Indian culture and ideas are also important functions of major Indian embassies. Shringla worked indefatigably on promoting them. He and his team organised International Yoga Day celebrations across the United States attended by tens of thousands of participants and also organised a series of events to commemorate the 550th birth anniversary of Guru Nanak, including a special commemorative event at the Hart Senate Office Building. The event was attended by US Senator Todd Young and US Representatives Judy Chu and Greg Pence. This was a part of a series of programmes that were organised around the United States by Consulates in association with diaspora and Sikh bodies.

Another major event in this sphere was a commemorative event at the Library of Congress in Washington, D.C., marking the 150th birth anniversary of Mahatma Gandhi. House Speaker Nancy Pelosi and India's External Affairs Minister, S. Jaishankar spoke at the event. The Library of Congress hosted a one-day exhibition on the life and teachings of Gandhi. The event was one of the many held across the country on October 2 to celebrate Gandhi's 150th birth anniversary. Speaker Pelosi, who was the Guest of Honour, expressed that the US House of Representatives had introduced a bipartisan resolution celebrating the 150th birthday of Gandhi, and his legacy.

The resolution—*S.Res.357—A resolution celebrating the 150th anniversary of the birth of Mahatma Gandhi*—was introduced by Indian American Rep. Raja Krishnamoorthi and was co-sponsored by, among others, Reps. George Holding, Brad Sherman, Joe Wilson, Gerry Connolly, Peter King, Ami Bera, Ro Khanna, Frank Pallone, Brenda Lawrence, Pete Olson, Pramila Jayapal, T. J. Cox, David Price and Ted Yoho. The Senate resolution was introduced by Sen. Bob Menendez.

Washington, D.C. is also the think tank capital of the world. He kept in touch with prominent think tanks and think tankers and spoke at several events. This made him a well-recognised figure in this circuit. Shringla also reached out to prominent figures in the public policy world such as Ambassador Nicholas Burns and Secretary William Cohen.

Shringla's eventful, and successful, tenure in the United States drew to an end when it was announced on December 23, 2019, that he would be appointed Foreign Secretary of India. He rapidly wound up his assignment with a series of parting engagements. He had the rare honour of a farewell call on President Donald Trump at the Oval Office of the White House before leaving the country. It was probably the first time that a US President had met an outgoing Indian Ambassador. This final meeting was a fitting end to the exceptional tenure of Harsh Shringla and his contribution to enhancing and strengthening India-US relations and paved the way for future strategic engagement.

10

FOREIGN SECRETARY

(January 2020-April 2022)

HARSH VARDAN SHRINGLA'S appointment as Ambassador to the United States brought him to the top of the diplomatic profession; his appointment as Foreign Secretary meant that he had ascended to the very pinnacle. He was now head of the Indian Foreign Service and the executive head of the Ministry of External Affairs. The Foreign Secretary of India holds a uniquely important position at many levels. India is one of the most consequential nations in the world, it is large in size, population, and in resources with one of the fastest-growing economies in the world. It has an influential global presence and is a major power on the trajectory to acquiring great power status. It is a country with global interests, and India's links with the world are accordingly complex and substantial. The Foreign Secretary is in some senses the linchpin of the government and national machinery that deals with all of India's interactions abroad. The territory, and the responsibility that come with it, are both vast. It is an ancient office and is in fact considered to be one of the great offices of the state. The "succession board" in the Foreign Secretary's office—in New Delhi's majestic South Block—lists predecessors going back to the mid-nineteenth century.

The Foreign Secretary is the chief diplomatic strategist and the chief professional diplomat of the government. He also oversees the instruments that execute diplomatic policies through the Ministry of External Affairs and its network of Embassies, High Commissions, Permanent Missions, Consulates General and other offices in almost 200 locations around the world. The Foreign Secretary, therefore, heads a massive arm of government and its only global arm. The Ministry of External Affairs also coordinates one of the largest consular operations globally responding to the needs of one of the great diasporas of the world. Through its development partnership operations, the Foreign Secretary also directs a large and growing portfolio of development projects, building schools, hospitals, and roads, among other things, on all continents. Yet another responsibility of the Foreign Secretary is to manage a transnational information and public diplomacy operation through traditional and digital channels.

Most government operations now have both inward and outward-facing components and require a whole-of-government approach. The Foreign Secretary is accordingly one of the principal cogs in the government's inter-agency process. The ceremonial aspect of diplomacy, with its pomp and pageantry and its rituals and its protocol, tends to involve the Foreign Secretary in some of its most important events.

The day-to-day work of the Foreign Secretary is demanding and punishing—almost superhuman. It comes long with an enormous number of "routine" functions and challenges. In addition, crises tend to erupt both regularly and unexpectedly. Agility and quick reflexes with an ability to think on one's feet are therefore essential. Shringla's considerable crisis management skills were taxed to the maximum due to the greatest shock that the world has faced since World War II, namely, the COVID-19 pandemic. It might be fair to say that no Foreign Secretary in the recent past has faced challenges of this magnitude.

The COVID-19 pandemic was a health catastrophe that delivered an enormous economic shock. The Ministry of External Affairs, like the rest of the government and society, was faced with an unprecedented situation. The disruptions caused by the pandemic have had a significant and continuing effect on a country like India, with its global presence and interests. Harsh Shringla managed the administrative and diplomatic response of the Ministry of External Affairs to this extraordinarily difficult challenge. The initial response—as it must be to all Black Swan events such as this—was necessarily ad hoc. However, as the pandemic persisted, the Ministry responded innovatively and effectively.

To begin with, the pandemic triggered lockdowns and bans on movements across the world. Millions of Indians and persons of Indian origin live outside India; hundreds and thousands of Indians are travelling abroad at any given time. These include, amongst others, students, professionals, workers and businessmen staying for varying lengths of time abroad. Hundreds of thousands of Indians were stranded across the world, and internal travel bans in several countries created further complications. In some countries, medicines and hospitals were restricted for use by locals only, while others were left to fend for themselves.

The Vande Bharat Mission (VBM)—possibly the largest evacuation exercise of its type in history—was launched with Shringla and the Ministry of External Affairs as one of its most important anchors. Indian Heads of Mission and Posts across the world were mobilised to reach out to stranded Indians, many of whom were, naturally, restive and worried.

Shringla began by constituting a COVID cell that formulated a plan to bring Indians back. The Ministry established a 24×7 communication centre to act as a single point of communication and a call centre for COVID-19 related queries from around the globe. The communication centre utilised telephone, email, and social media to answer queries, resolve problems, disseminate information and act as a clearing-house and coordination centre. Internal chains of command and jurisdiction were reoriented to increase bandwidth. Capacities were scaled up.

Stranded Indians were "mapped" through a custom-built portal. A very difficult exercise of assigning priorities to passengers was conducted. This portal and its data were made available to all stakeholders, especially the relevant Ministries/Departments, State Governments and Missions which were involved in the welfare of the returning persons. A real-time picture was developed on the basis of which flights were planned to specific locations in India in different States from multiple points of origin abroad. State governments, immigration and health officials accordingly planned logistics such as screening, testing, quarantine and transportation for arriving passengers. Coordination with State governments was critical in ensuring that Indians returned to their domiciles in the most economic and quick manner. Shringla personally briefed State Chief Secretaries about the Vande Bharat Mission operations and thereafter designated senior Ministry officers as nodal officers for coordination with specific States.

It must be remembered that this operation took place in an atmosphere in which States were preoccupied with the inter-State movement of migrant workers and were faced with the dilemma of allowing stranded Indians to return home, while migrant workers at home were still held back and facing hardship. The flights, however, commenced on May 7, 2020, and State governments, Missions and central government agencies adapted swiftly. Air India worked out 64 flights for Phase-I of the Mission. Passenger manifests were determined in advance by missions and careful coordination ensured a smooth operation. Indians also began to move back through land border check-posts with Nepal, Bhutan and Bangladesh. A number of them were also brought back by sea. The growing demand for flights from Indians stranded abroad far outstripped Air India's capacity. Shringla and the Ministry then worked to develop Standard Operating Procedures and policies for Charter flights.

He ensured that missions abroad extended all possible assistance to the stranded Indians after COVID-19 related restrictions were imposed. The assistance varied based on the needs of the people. Missions set up 24×7 COVID-19 emergency helplines for all kinds of assistance to Indian nationals in need. In some countries, Indian nationals were provided with masks and sanitisers, food kits, preliminary medical consultation, along with aid, boarding & lodging, and even tickets in the most deserving cases.

The critical phase of repatriation of stranded Indians continued until December 2020. Eventually, they gave way to international flights under bilateral "Air Bubble" arrangements with several countries. In all, Shringla and his team worked successfully on coordinating 9 phases of the Vande Bharat Mission by end-February 2021. Simultaneously, he and his team also worked on outbound evacuation operations. The complicated movements of foreigners of many nationalities, stranded in all parts of India, travelling to many destinations from multiple locations in India were organised.

The COVID-19 pandemic hit India in several "waves". The waves caused rapid increases in the number of cases and in the demand for medical services and medical products. The country faced severe shortfalls in respect of medical products and essential medical supplies. Procurement of medical products and essential medical supplies from the global market was one of the responsibilities assigned to the Foreign Secretary and his team. This required a major international effort involving Indian diplomatic missions in several countries.

Healthcare is a highly globalised industry and medical products and supplies are produced by global supply chains. Sourcing such products and supplies during a pandemic, therefore, were by necessity a global effort. Ventilators, PPE kits, N95 masks, 3-ply surgical masks and testing kits were sourced from several countries. This partly helped India meet its demand for medical devices and masks, especially when domestic manufacturing of these items had not picked up the scale.

While the first wave peaked in September 2020, the second wave peaked in April and May 2021. The shortage of critical medical supplies such as oxygen during the second wave had catastrophic consequences. Shringla and his team were asked to mount a global effort to source Liquid Medical Oxygen and other essential medical supplies such as drugs like Remdesivir within hours. The Liquid Medical Oxygen that was sourced had to be shipped from international points of origin to locations across India. It was an effort that involved multiple stakeholders—public and private—larger quantities and more complex logistics. Shringla and the Ministry had to create policies and standard operating procedures on the go to manage the inflows of supplies. This massive effort succeeded in bringing in critical volume after tackling major supply chains issues such as cryogenic tankers and oxygen cylinders. It also sourced zeolites, oxygen concentrators, and oxygen plants Remdesivir, Tocilizumab, Amphotericin and Isavuconazole.

Vaccines have played a key role in the response to the pandemic. India, because of the size and capacity of its indigenous vaccine industry, is a major player in this respect. The Foreign Secretary and his team worked on this vaccination drive at many levels. He and the Ministry facilitated access to vaccines, vaccine technology and vaccine raw material for Indian entities. They also managed important aspects of outward-facing vaccine-related initiatives such as Vaccine Maitri and the Quad vaccine initiative. Subsequently, he was also involved in taking the Indian vaccine, Covaxin and the Indian CoWIN app, globally. This involved regulatory processes in several countries and organisations such as the World Health Organisation.

The pandemic was not just a healthcare and economic shock. It is also a significant geopolitical event. Amongst other things, it established that crises of this nature require more, and not less, international cooperation. The Ministry, and Harsh Shringla, took active roles in a number of initiatives that placed India in a leadership role in global efforts to combat COVID-19. This included diplomatic initiatives in multilateral and plurilateral platforms such as SAARC, G20, WHO and WTO. The QUAD undertook a number of pandemic-related activities as did BRICS. Shringla and the Ministry also focused on issues such as a TRIPS waiver for vaccines and related products.

Vaccines were not the only Indian product that had an international demand. Early in the pandemic, India's domestic pharmaceutical industry had become the centre of global attention due to its production capacity for drugs such as paracetamol, hydroxychloroquine (HCQ) and azithromycin. With the support of the Ministry, Shringla, coordinated a massive operation to transport large quantities of such medicines as humanitarian grants and commercial exports to more than a hundred countries.

The creation of Rapid Response Teams to move swiftly to aid countries to deal with the pandemic in India's extended neighbourhood is not often spoken of. Those I spoke to narrate how Shringla worked closely with the then Chief of Defence Staff, late General Bipin Rawat, with whom he had an excellent rapport. They set up teams of military doctors and paramedics with equipment and medicines to travel at short notice to locations such Kuwait, Maldives, Mauritius, Seychelles and Comoros. These were done through a number of seaborne and airborne operations that delivered expertise and supplies through Mission SAGAR and Operation Sanjeevani.

The geopolitics and geo-economics that drive diplomatic equations did not cease to operate during the pandemic. Harsh Shringla had to continue to play the role of diplomatic strategist and operational manager.

His major challenge was to move the business of diplomacy to the digital domain which he with the support of his team were able to do with remarkable rapidity. The Prime Minister and External Affairs Minister conducted virtual meetings with Indian Ambassadors and officers. Diplomatic meetings, both multilateral and bilateral, moved to the digital domain, with virtual summits, virtual ministerial and virtual senior officers' meetings and consultations.

The lockdown happened less than two months after Mr. Shringla took over as Foreign Secretary. During this brief period, diplomacy was at the hectic pace that New Delhi was accustomed to. He took over as Foreign Secretary on January 29, 2020. The month of February 2020 saw incoming visits from President Donald Trump, the President of Portugal, the President of Myanmar, the Vice President of Vietnam, Prime Minister Mahinda Rajapakse of Sri Lanka, Deputy Prime Minister Winston Peters of New Zealand, and a number of African Defence Ministers for the India-Africa Defence Ministers Conclave. The visit of President Trump was a high-voltage spectacle that culminated in the historic "Namaste Trump" meeting at the Narendra Modi Stadium in Ahmedabad on February 24, 2020. At least 100,000 people attended this event which took place five months after Howdy Modi in Houston. Harsh Shringla—first as Ambassador to the United States, and now as Foreign Secretary—was involved in crafting and executing both these enormous public diplomacy events. This was the dizzying pace of an average of a Head of State or Government visiting Delhi every week.

A Foreign Secretary is expected to have his own schedule of visits. Shringla's priorities and his focus became clear with his first outbound visit. He chose Afghanistan as the destination. He visited Kabul on February 28-29, 2020. According to the Ministry of External Affairs Press Release for this occasion, it "was his first visit abroad after taking over as India's Foreign Secretary one month back and highlights the strategic partnership between the two countries."

The events of the next month were equally intense but of a different nature. The pandemic had begun to disrupt travel. Diplomatic action shifted to the virtual space. With the benefit of hindsight, it is now obvious that gears shifted quickly. Within the space of the month of March, Prime Minister Modi had telephonic conversations with Prime Minister Netanyahu of Israel, Prime Minister Boris Johnson, the Crown Prince of Saudi Arabia, the Amir of Qatar, the Prime Minister of Abu Dhabi, President Putin and the President of the European Commission. The first virtual summits were also convened. Prime Minister Modi interacted with leaders of SAARC countries by video on March 16. He then attended an Extraordinary Virtual G20 Leaders' Summit on March 26. Diplomacy had gone virtual within a month. Shringla and the Ministry of External Affairs adapted and innovated with speed and agility. Internal methods and processes in the Ministry, which had developed over decades, had to adjust to the new virtual reality in weeks, if not days. Prime Minister Modi first spoke to Indian Heads of Missions by video on March 30.

The fact that the COVID-19 Cell was also created during this period hints at the frenetic pace of activity. The Ministry of External Affairs website further lists a call between Shringla and his "Indo-Pacific counterparts" on March 20, 2020. The Press Release for this says that this was "A telephonic conference call initiated by U.S. Deputy Secretary of State Stephen Biegun for discussions among some countries in the Indo-Pacific region on issues related to countering COVID-19. The teleconference included senior representatives from Australia, the Republic of Korea, Vietnam, New Zealand, and Japan." His first visit to Afghanistan and this conversation with Indo-Pacific colleagues gave an indication of the emerging geopolitical focus of Indian foreign policy in Shringla's time.

The pandemic, which is a Black Swan event, has highlighted this ongoing geopolitical transition and the "inadequacies of the current structure and thinking". Shringla has been fairly explicit about the guiding principles of Indian foreign policy during this period of flux and movement. One theme runs through many of his statements and remarks—the theme of continuity and change. To him foreign policy is not made in a vacuum; geography, he has often said, is destiny. Indian foreign policy would necessarily have to build on the experience of the past while adapting to the currents of the present.

A major challenge that Indian foreign policy faces is navigating what has been described as "rebalancing". Speaking to Vivekananda International Foundation on "Global Rebalancing and India's Foreign Policy" in June 2021, Foreign Secretary Shringla asserted how the post-World War II international order was rapidly changing and how "mainstream concepts of globalization" created by the United Nations Charter, the Bretton Woods Institutions, the G7, the Uruguay Round of GATT, and the Montreal Protocol were being challenged. He added that, "the rapid growth of Asia's share in global economic output, the business acumen of Asian companies and their growing revenues, and the growing salience of Asian technological prowess is driving a shift in the global economic centre of gravity and the transition is manifest in the waning of the "unipolar moment" following the end of the Cold War and in the emergence of a multipolar world. The transition is also manifest in doubts about the continuing relevance of the existing structures and pillars to contemporary problems."

According to him, India's response would be with a multipolar focus. As India, and its immediate Asian environment, are both multipolar, the existing policies like "Neighbourhood First, Act East and Think West" were being revitalised. To him, the other major drivers of Indian foreign policy are SAGAR—Security and Growth for All in the Region—and an Indo-Pacific strategy. The main elements of the Indo-Pacific strategy were articulated by Prime Minister Narendra Modi at the Shangri La dialogue in Singapore in June 2018. These include a free, open and inclusive order in the Indo-Pacific that is based on "ASEAN-Centrality".

At the Launch of the First Yoga App before the International Day of Yoga, 2015

With the Late Tanuja Gyabaka whom Harsh Shringla as Ambassador Helped out of a Tight Spot in Bangkok

In the Field: High Commissioner Harsh Shringla Delivering Humanitarian Assistance in Bangladesh

Harsh Shringla with Prime Minister Sheikh Hasina of Bangladesh

Father and Son: Ashoka and Harsh Shringla at the Redwood Forest, California

With Indian Origin Astronaut Sunita Williams at NASA Houston, May 2019

At a Meeting at the White House with President of the United States, Donald Trump in 2019

External Affairs Minister Dr S Jaishankar, US House of Representatives Speaker Nancy Pelosi and Ambassador Harsh Shringla, Washington DC

First Lady Laura Bush, President George W Bush, Ambassador Harsh Shringla, Consul General Anupam Ray, Dallas

External Affairs Minister Dr S Jaishankar, Prime Minister Narendra Modi, Foreign Secretary Vijay Gokhale and Ambassador Harsh Shringla at Howdy Modi

Author with Foreign Secretary Harsh Shringla

Foreign Secretary Harsh Shringla with Russian Foreign Minister Lavrov

Foreign Secretary Harsh Shringla in Moscow – February 2022

Foreign Secretary Harsh Shringla Casting His Vote as President of the United Nations Security Council on Afghanistan

Foreign Secretary Shringla with His Holiness the Dalai Lama

Son of the Soil

As Chief Guest at the Prize Giving Ceremony of Mayo College, Ajmer in 2021

With Prime Minister Shri Narendra Modi

India would also maintain "comprehensive strategic relations with major powers while maintaining strategic autonomy". As Foreign Secretary, Shringla engaged extensively with the United States during his tenure, balancing strategic alliances with Russia, the United Kingdom and France.

With regard to China, India has in the recent past faced serious challenges on the Line of Actual Control (LAC). Lives were lost on this border after over 40 years and Shringla postulates that India is "engaged with China both through the military and diplomatic channels on this, and remain firmly committed to resolving all outstanding issues through dialogue".

The other developments have been the QUAD, and the first QUAD Summit between India, the United States, Japan and Australia, which have received much attention. Shringla placed this in perspective in his remarks at an India Investor Summit organised by banking giant, J. P. Morgan in September 2021. He said that "the agenda of cooperation under the QUAD framework is constructive and diverse. The four QUAD countries are engaged on issues of connectivity and infrastructure, emerging technologies, climate action, education, and most important of all, COVID-19 responses—which include vaccines collaboration, and resilient and reliable supply chains."

To Shringla India is a country with an expanding economy, competent leadership, aspirations and entrepreneurial energy. It has an ever-expanding global footprint and matters more than before. India is also a country on a growth trajectory and it would matter even more in the future. As globalisation meant that no country was alone. India, more than many others, is a country with global interests. Speaking to the Indian Council of World Affairs a few months after taking over as Foreign Secretary, he said that the "Indian economy, and therefore the material well-being, is plugged into global supply chains", where "we view the world as a borderless economy with an interlinked marketplace".

Since common global problems require common solutions, one of Mr. Shringla's focus areas was to ensure a coherence and strategic focus in India's increasing multilateral diplomatic initiatives. India was on the UN Security Council for a non-permanent tenure. It has just completed its tenure chairing BRICS and is currently President of Shanghai Cooperation Organisation (SCO) and the G20. As someone who has spent a decade of his career on multilateral work at various levels, many of his colleagues point out that Shringla was a rare Foreign Secretary who was comfortable dealing with the multilateral complexities that came his way, It was therefore of some satisfaction to him that he was at the helm during India's non-permanent tenure at the UN Security Council. After having spent year (2002-6) at the margins of the Security Council as political officer in the Permanent Mission of India to the UN in New York, Shringla felt that he had come full-circle when, as President of the Security Council, he oversaw the adoption of the UN's seminal resolution on Afghanistan (UNSCR 2593).

He considers it a challenging period for multilateralism as it has faced unprecedented stresses due to the pandemic. India in these circumstances would be guided by what Prime Minister Narendra Modi has described as human-centric globalisation. It focused on the "collective well-being of humankind and having multilateral fora focus on promoting the shared interests of humanity". It also focused on "the need to put human beings at the centre of our vision of global prosperity and cooperation".

One of the areas which did pose a challenge and to which he devoted time and personal attention was climate change. The issue of how India should approach the COP26 Summit at Glasgow was debated extensively in inter-ministerial processes. It is significant that Prime Minister Modi made bold and far reaching commitments under the Panchamrit at Glasgow. It demonstrated India's global leadership and its resolve to move conclusively towards a cleaner and greener future in its best interest and, in doing so, contributing to the future of humanity in sync with India's ancient philosophy of Vasudaiva Kuttumbakam.

Another concept that appears frequently in Shringla's remarks, is that of being *atmanirbhar*. He describes it as strategic autonomy, and "believes that centres of power and gravity in the current international system are diversifying, growing and shifting. New players such as non-state actors and business interests have created entirely new diplomatic domains and are often more influential than many nation-states. India's interests, like those of other players, in such a fluid environment, will constantly shift. The comforts of belonging to a bloc—or avoiding it—are gone." Strategic autonomy and human-centric globalisation, thus, mean more diplomatic interaction and not less.

Harsh Shringla came to the Foreign Secretary's position with an unusual depth and variety of multilateral experience. It was to prove in handy in managing this major thrust on multilateral and plurilateral initiatives. The normative framework of India's Security Council presidency was based on the concept of "Reformed Multilateralism", and it points out that contemporary global challenges cannot be fought with outdated structures. In the absence of comprehensive reforms, the UN faces a crisis of confidence. A reformed multilateralism is needed that reflects today's realities, gives voice to all stakeholders, addresses contemporary challenges and focuses on human welfare. All this meant that much more was expected of the Ministry of External Affairs and the Indian Foreign Service.

Some of Shringla's administrative decisions as Foreign Secretary are quite striking. It is well known that the Ministry of External Affairs has a lean staffing structure. Shringla met the unprecedented pressures of the situation with the available leadership, manpower and resources. He focused on identifying broad challenges and then delegated authority and created empowered structures that could find solutions. This freed them to take strategic calls and devote attention to problems that were escalated to that level. He also adopted a unique matrix structure like that of start-ups. The chain of command and hierarchy were made flexible and were oriented to solving problems. He was able to create a "surge" capacity that scaled up literally overnight.

His ability to take everyone along was on full display. Networks were created to bring all stakeholders together. He was also able to break down silos within the Ministry. He took decisions quickly and used technology wherever he could, customised portals were created and video and communication technology were used to great effect. His ability to think on his feet was also fully evident as policies had to be created, sometimes at hours' notice, to deal with the demands of the pandemic.

Through all this, Shringla was able to rally, through his quiet but determined leadership, along with the Ministry and his team. Dispersed across the world, facing multiple lockdowns and disruptions, and in the face of complexities and difficulties, Shringla's team "held the line".

11

THOUGHTS ON INDIA'S FOREIGN POLICY

IN HARSH SHRINGLA'S view, foreign policy represents the national interest of a State in its engagement and interaction with other countries. It is how a State can optimise its national interests. It is not a static concept. It is not something that remains as it is. It is constantly evolving and changing as it adapts to the changing geopolitical situation and the needs of the time. Foreign policy by its very nature has to be adaptable, and responsive. At the same time, it has to be crafted with great care and caution. Foreign policy cannot be about maintaining the status quo. It has to continuously change and adapt in accordance with the shifting tides and sands of international fortunes. This imposes upon the practitioners of foreign policy and upon those who guide and influence foreign policy the requirement to constantly improve their comprehension, and understanding of the international situation and of national options. This understanding and comprehension is necessary for them to be able to guide foreign policy in a manner that best suits the interest of the country.

For Harsh Shringla foreign policy needs to have immediate, mid-term and long-term goals. He thinks that when viewed with a long-term perspective, India's foreign policy, by and large, has been consistent. India always believed in a certain level of strategic autonomy. It has kept away from military alliances. It has avoided large blocks and prefers not to take sides in geopolitical divides. It tries not to see the world in North-South or East-West binaries.

India has tried to situate itself in a multipolar world. It is conscious of its economic growth and its evolving status as a regional and global power. At the same time, India has always tried to work on the basis of equal engagement between all states. India prefers a multilateral system that reflects the realities of a multipolar world, rather than unipolar or bipolar global orders.

In the mid-term, Harsh Shringla believes that India will witness significant changes in the geopolitical situation. The global centre of gravity—political, economic and technological—will shift towards Asia, and therefore to the Indo-Pacific region. These changing geopolitics according to Shringla has created a disruptive dynamic. Alterations in the status quo have always resulted in some disequilibrium. As a result, differences, friction, and even conflict between states are more likely and will require to be actively anticipated, managed and contained.

In the short term, he asserts that India has to look at the immediate consequences of the changing geopolitics in its neighbourhood. The rise of China, which is already the second largest economy, and is on its way to becoming the largest economy in the world, will create challenges. China possesses increasing military strength. It is investing additional resources in an expansive military build-up. It is expanding the PLA Navy, its Air Force and the PLA itself. This massive growth in military capacity, he thinks, will impact India and larger global politics.

India has already felt the impact of these changes. Its security has been affected by the clashes on the border with China. It has seen a determined effort by China to increase its influence in India's neighbourhood. A growing nexus—or even collusion—between Pakistan and China is a reality.

This requires India to keep its lines of communication and engagement open with its traditional and new partners. It needs to carefully tend its equations with its partners such as the United States, Japan, Australia, and Europe, even while maintaining its partnership with old friends such as Russia.

Harsh Shringla feels that Indian diplomacy has been very adept at creating new groupings, new alliances, new diplomatic constructs and new platforms. India has substantially augmented its relationship with its extended neighbourhood—with Southeast Asia, Central Asia, the Gulf countries, Africa, the Pacific Islands states, and with Indian Ocean states. It has made enormous progress in mutually beneficial engagement with states in all these regions. An India-Central Asia Summit, the new QUAD or I2U2 (India, Israel, UAE, USA), and new relationships in the Gulf are some relatively new initiatives. India has developed excellent relations in Africa. It has invested in the development of the African continent. India shares excellent relations with the ASEAN countries and has developed good synergies. For example, India is cooperating with Vietnam in the oil and gas sector. It is working with Indonesia in port development. It has expanded defence cooperation with the Philippines and recently concluded a US$375 million defence deal involving supply of Brahmos missiles. Australia is now an increasingly important partner within the QUAD and other multilateral constructs. All of these indicative engagements point to a significant broadening of diplomatic horizons in the recent past. They also indicate that India has not been constrained by challenges. It has exploited them to increase its diplomatic space and capital.

Harsh Shringla feels that one of India's greatest assets in these endeavours has been the Prime Minister's own stature and personality. Prime Minister Modi has travelled to many of these countries and made personal efforts to expand these relationships. He recalls a discussion on the United Arab Emirates in which it became clear that the Prime Minister's own personal relationship with the Crown Prince of UAE is the major driver of the growing bilateral engagement. One concrete example of the importance of this personal relationship is the six-fold increase in UAE's investments in India in the last seven years. Thus, Shringla considers personal relations to be extremely significant in developing the overall relationship with any country.

The Ministry of External Affairs has a major contribution in these processes. Under the Prime Minister's overall leadership and direction, the Ministry, headed by External Affairs Minister and staffed by the Indian Foreign Service, acts as the external arm of the government. Harsh Shringla feels that high-quality human resources that enable implementation of the Prime Minister's and External Affairs Minister's vision are very important. Shringla asserts that today India has one of the best diplomatic services in the world. It is, however, given India's growing regional and global presence, comparatively small. Each Indian diplomat handles a volume of work and responsibility that would, in other similar countries, be assigned to two or three diplomats. Consequently, Indian diplomats have no alternative to working extremely hard to multitask. In the course of his career and his postings he has witnessed a manifold increase in the responsibilities of foreign service officers and what is required of them. They continue to steadily increase. Indian diplomats have not only shouldered these increasing responsibilities, they have succeeded in producing results. In other words, they have delivered and continue to deliver.

He gives the example of the 'Azadi ka Mahotsav' celebrations. The largest number of events to celebrate the 75th anniversary of India's independence has been held by Indian missions abroad. A total of 7,000 recorded events have been conducted by missions all over the world to commemorate this national landmark the activities range from having iconic buildings painted and lit up in India's colours to significant discourses on India's development and progress in cutting-edge areas like digital diplomacy, start-ups, innovations, etc.

Harsh Shringla feels that the IFS and the Ministry of External Affairs represent a country that has changed much since he joined. The new India is for practical purposes a different country. One reflection of India's growing salience in the world stage is its increasing contribution to global governance systems. Shringla points to India's recently concluded non-permanent membership of the United Nations Security Council. In the last two years, India has chaired the UNSC twice. It has, during this period, also presided over BRICS, the Shanghai Cooperation Organization (SCO), and then went on to take over the G20 Presidency.

During its UNSC presidencies, India has in a Security Council first highlighted the importance of dealing with the challenge of maritime security in a holistic manner. It has used its BRICS and SCO presidencies to highlight other concerns. India's presidency of the G20 is highly significant both for India and the group. The G20 represents the largest economies in the world. It represents 80% of the Global GDP, 75% of international trade, and 60% of the world's population. Harsh Shringla believes that, today, it is perhaps one of the most significant groupings anywhere in the world. He compares the UN Security Council to a club and the G20 to an association of countries that have proven capacities.

Shringla feels that the Security Council is frozen in time and needs to be reformed. Its five permanent members are the five victors of World War II. This archaic formula needs to be changed to represent current realities. India has always been vocal about the need to reform the UNSC and believes that the inclusion of India as a permanent member is necessary for the Security Council to continue to be relevant.

Ideology, according to Shringla, is important. It is always important to have a set of beliefs and an outlook. They should not be rigid, however. An ideology should not weigh the country down. Today, many people question the ideology of the 1950s and 1960s and even the 1970s. Indian foreign policy today, according to Shringla, is much more supple and adept in responding to the needs of the times. It is a more pragmatic, more realistic foreign policy that is closely based on its national interest. He thinks that it is probably because those who represent India now are closer to the needs and aspirations of the people of India. Demographically, India is today a young country with 60% of its population below 35 years of age. He believes that the younger Indian generation is an aspirational generation who lives in a more prosperous, more developed, upwardly mobile and rising country. They expect that their leadership will respond to their aspiration and deliver to them the opportunities that they need.

Reflecting on the issues that are important for Indian diplomacy today, Harsh Shringla feels that it should look beyond managing foreign policy and the relations between states. It should have a focus on the welfare and well-being of Indian nationals. Indian nationals are globally mobile. They study abroad, work abroad and live abroad. One example of how the Indian diplomatic apparatus is responding to these new priorities is the finalisation of a series of mobility and migration partnership agreements with a number of countries like the UK and Portugal. These agreements—along with efforts to focus on Japan and some other countries—are creating opportunities for Indian nationals abroad. India wants its nationals, Indian professionals, and trained and skilled manpower, to be the preferred human resources in the global market. Shringla believes that the nature of the demographic changes in many parts of the world will create situations in a few decades where Indian professionals provide the economic backbone of countries. He recalls one of the discussions with the

UAE about creating end-to-end solutions for manpower requirements, including by training and skilling Indians to adapt to the requirements of that country.

Continuing on issues of contemporary importance, Harsh Shringla believes that India can also leverage the expertise it has gained through Digital India. The creation of digital platforms and digital pathways for delivery of services has been transformational. For example, NREGA (National Rural Employment Guarantee Act) beneficiaries never imagined that they would receive money directly into their bank accounts. Direct Benefits Transfers that are "cashless" deposits into bank accounts opened under the "Pradhan Mantri Jan Dhan Yojana" have brought 300 to 400 million people directly into the formal economy. In this context, it could be argued that although the government's demonetisation policy was criticised, it catalysed the growth of a cashless economy in India. This has also led to other innovations and to conversations about digital currencies and blockchain technologies. These are indicative of a mindset, one in which technology is being used to improve transparency and functioning. One of the interesting examples he gave was that of the discovery of almost 17 million "Benami" accounts (accounts of the people who never existed) after the introduction of these measures.

Harsh Shringla gave the example of the global conference on the CoWIN organised by the Ministry of External Affairs and the Ministry of Health in which 42 countries participated. The CoWIN digital platform has been used by India to successfully administer 2 billion vaccines to Indian citizens. Citizens can access the CoWIN app to obtain their vaccination records and for certification. He pointed out that this is an open-source, safe and scalable system that can be used anywhere in the world. This is how India is using "data for development". The idea that data should be available for the common good and not be utilised solely for profit underlies the kind of initiative that India is spearheading in the G20. Shringla believes that the G20 presidency is an opportunity for

India to create a visible imprint of an India that wants to make and can make a difference.

The development of the CoWIN app and a growing ecosystem around the cashless economy is the product of an India that is at the cutting edge of developing digital technologies, of innovation, and of a start-up culture. Shringla feels that India is on its way to being a world leader. The deployment of world-class human resources and managerial ability to ensure an exponential increase in the generation of power from renewable sources and to create a world-class infrastructure network through the "Gati Shakti" programme will have massive downstream impact.

India is a country that is in mission mode. Projecting these attitudinal changes, leveraging these new capacities, and articulating and transmitting the vision of the Prime Minister at a global level is, Shringla feels, one of the primary tasks of the Ministry of External Affairs.

Another issue about which Harsh Shringla feels strongly, and on which he acted during his tenure as Foreign Secretary, is about making foreign policy intelligible to the common man. He feels that the functioning and priorities of the Ministry of External Affairs has always been shrouded in some level of mystery. Foreign policy exponents have always talked a language that the common man could not understand. Shringla has attempted to change this by talking in the lexicon and language of the layman. He feels strongly that foreign policy must be relevant to the actual requirements of the common man.

Speaking at a global lecture organised by the Department of International Relations, Sikkim University on April 2, 2021, he spoke extensively about how changes in Indian visa policy during his tenure as High Commissioner of India in Bangladesh had a direct impact on tourism in Sikkim. Tourism inflows in Sikkim increased by 90% after people from foreign countries—people with spending power—were allowed to visit Sikkim. This put Sikkim on the map for people with the resources to come and make a difference to India's domestic economy.

When he was in his hometown Darjeeling for a charity programme on November 21, 2021, he gave the example of the reopening of the "Chilhati-Haldibari Express" railway route between India and Bangladesh. This was the original route of the Darjeeling Mail train between Kolkata and Siliguri through modern-day Bangladesh. It was interrupted after the 1965 India-Pakistan war. The Darjeeling Mail was then rerouted over the Farakka Barrage. Harsh Shringla believes that the reopening of this route points to the potential of the future. He feels that the opening of this route means that a Dhaka-Siliguri train line can possibly become a reality in the future. Such a railway connection, if and when it materialises, will integrate the region and benefit both Indian states and Bangladesh. Shringla pointed to the enormous economic significance of a country like Bangladesh in the vicinity of Sikkim and the Darjeeling area. It is a nation with 160 million people with 6 per cent to 8 per cent economic growth, increasing spending power and with good social-economic development indices. It has an increasing number of people with growing disposable income who are very keen to see the world. The closest place to them, and one to which they all want to travel, is Darjeeling and Sikkim. A train will make it much more accessible and will have the impact of growing the tourism and travel industries and injecting much needed cash into the local economy.

He also spoke of the direct relevance of two of the fundamental pillars of Indian foreign policy, the "Neighbourhood First Policy" and "Act East Policy" for the people of this region. The Siliguri corridor links the North East to India and therefore provides the land connectivity between India and East and South-East Asia. It connects India to Bangladesh, Nepal, and Bhutan and further down, to Myanmar and Thailand. It also connects these countries to each other through India. Siliguri and, therefore, Darjeeling, have a geostrategic location. They are an important crossroads for India and for the greater region. This has the potential of transforming the entire area. Shringla feels that it is important for the people of this region and for institutions to create capacities. He also feels that it is important to involve people in the effort so that they develop equities in the implementation of the Neighbourhood First and Act East Policies. He gave an example of the cooperation with Japan in capacity building projects in Sikkim and other North-Eastern states.

Harsh Shringla emphasises the importance of the 3Ts—Trade, Tourism and Technology—for Indian diplomacy. Prime Minister Modi has himself emphasised the importance of these 3Ts. The Ministry of External Affairs has accordingly directed all its embassies to focus on the promotion of these objectives, namely, how to promote greater trade, how to promote greater inflows of tourists, and how to access the best technology for India. In the case of the third T—technology—the emphasis is on promoting a two-way flow. Shringla recalled that he had instructed all embassies that the entire embassy—and not just its commercial wings—should focus on these 3Ts. This should be the focus of all officers from Ambassador down, and he had made it clear that their performance evaluations would be based on their work on these parameters. He thinks that these priorities have to seep into the work of a Ministry which has hitherto been largely focused on the political aspects of diplomacy.

The country has set itself a target of US$2 trillion in exports by 2030 and the Ministry of External Affairs must play a role in making this a reality. The target of US$400 billion that was earlier set has been exceeded. During his time as Foreign Secretary, Shringla played an active role in this process by mobilising Embassies. They worked, among other things, on Free Trade Agreements, on market promotion activities, on working with private sector exporters, and on tackling market access issues.

Shringla has always been interested in the promotion of tourism. Whether as the Commercial Counsellor at Indian Embassy in Paris, or in Israel, he has always worked on promoting tourism. He recalls his experience in Israel where he found considerable potential in promotion of India as a destination. A certain number of young Israelis had a keen interest in visiting India but this segment was not all. High-end tourism from Israel was a possibility that could produce good results. This has since become reality. This is in addition to the tourism focus of his work in Bangladesh which has been written about earlier.

Shringla's views on the importance of technology for India have already been described. He also feels strongly about the role of Embassies and diplomats in promoting access to technologies that can benefit India. When he was Ambassador to the United States, his emphasis was on science and technology. He worked closely with specialist diplomats such as the Science and Technology Counsellor, and Space Counsellor. He connected with key US high-tech players such as NASA. He visited NASA in Houston to identify and access technologies that are required by ISRO and identify areas where both could work together. These initiatives have helped immensely and today ISRO engagement with the USA and other countries has increased significantly. ISRO has received considerable help from the Ministry of External Affairs in connecting with counterparts and partners who can provide ISRO with the inputs that are necessary to make India's space programmes successful.

Technology flows, it has been pointed out earlier, are bi-directional. The Ministry of External Affairs also ensures that there is more joint communication, more research, more exchanges and more sharing of India's technology with its neighbours. The South Asian Satellite project, for example, is the Prime Minister's vision to have a satellite that caters to and provides free services to our South Asian neighbours, including remote sensing for climate and crop development.

Harsh Shringla believes that there is a lot that is yet to be done. In his words, the cup is never full as there is always something more than one can do. He feels that what is important is that one should never stop working to achieve one's national aims and objectives. In his words: "I keep telling my colleagues in our service that you have joined a service. What you're doing is providing a service to the nation. I worked in the private sector and in the public sector. I could have stayed there if I wanted to. If my only aim was to get remuneration, then I could have looked elsewhere. But you joined public service because you wanted to make a difference—and here is the opportunity to make a difference. So, the harder you work, the more result-oriented you are, the more benefits you bring in tangible terms to your country in whatever you do. That is the most significant contribution and that is really what we should do. For anybody to say that I have done enough, or to say that I have achieved what I had to, I think would be wrong. It is never enough and you can always do more."

This has always been Harsh Shringla's way of thinking. He has constantly pushed himself and pushed others working with him to achieve more, do more, and produce better results. That is what he has done his entire working life.

12

CONCLUSION

HARSH SHRINGLA'S life has been one of evolution and constant improvement. He was not the brightest student in school. He strove to perform better in academics and in extra-curricular activities in university. He succeeded. He stood second in Delhi University in his 2nd-year examinations and emerged in the top bracket of his class in the Honours examination, much to the surprise of some of his professors. He also earned the coveted College Colours in Hockey in his first year and participated in a number of mountaineering expeditions.

Many years later, he was recognized for his merit by both his school and college. His school, Mayo College, presented him with the JT Gibson Award for Outstanding Alumni in 2017 and invited him as Chief Guest at the annual Prize Giving ceremony. His College (St. Stephen's) invited him to address the students on the occasion of Founders' Day and formally inducted him into the Order of Illustrious Stephanians.

By the time he completed his degree and was ready to seek employment, he had already honed himself into an impressive personality. His success in the interview and group discussion processes in three highly sought-after companies was testimony to his newly acquired abilities.

In the Indian Foreign Service, Harsh Shringla gave his very best to every assignment and every post he occupied. His career moved steadily along an ascending trajectory. His abilities and suitability for high office became increasingly evident at every step of the ladder. Whether it was his being selected as Joint Secretary for a prestigious neighbourhood division, and later becoming one of the youngest Indian Ambassadors to Thailand, Bangladesh and the USA, it became apparent that he was on a path to assuming the highest office in the Indian Foreign Service—that of Foreign Secretary.

What accounts for this extraordinary rise of someone who comes from an obscure corner of Darjeeling in North Bengal? How did this man with humble but devoted parents, and a complete absence of any influence or support, progress to this level? The answer may lie in the way he has moulded himself. He has always believed in complete focus and dedication to his work. Everything else has been secondary to this subjective, sometimes to his detriment. Secondly, he has also always done what is right and never hesitated to take decisions that others would have preferred to avoid. This resulted in some differences of opinion with some of his seniors but later, as he assumed positions of independence in decision-making, this sense of doing what is right, or *nishkama karma*, produced the desired results. Thirdly, Shringla has always worked to make government services as freely and easily accessible as possible in the larger public interest. In Thailand, he started for the first time an Open House, where any member of the Indian community could come and seek redressal on the many consular-related issues that were pending before the Embassy. He ensured that there were no outstanding issues that could not be resolved in the normal course with the Embassy when he left. He continued this policy in Bangladesh and the USA. In the case of the former, his greatest contribution was to ensure that access to genuine visa seekers was made into a smooth and hassle-free process. Pendency was removed and the number of visas issued in a single year increased from 5 lakh to 15 lakh, thereby removing a major irritant in the people-to-people ties and bringing in tourist revenues in excess of US$ 4 billion to India. In the US, he continued the Open-Door policy, meeting Indian community associations and students in all of the 22 states that he travelled to during his short stint as Ambassador in that country.

More importantly, Harsh Shringla always ensured that those who have worked with him have been amply looked after and suitably recognised for their work and contribution. Whether it relates to a Multi-Tasking Staff (MTS) member who died while on duty in his office or an officer who performed beyond the normal call of duty in one of his stations abroad, he had always put the needs of his colleagues before his own.

On his return to Delhi as Foreign Secretary, Shringla ensured that accommodation for the youngest officers was available when he created additional housing capacity. He also brought in a system that allowed young officers to opt for an area of work of their preference in the Ministry. This was in sharp contrast to the ad hoc allocation of work when an officer first returned to Delhi.

Harsh Shringla has enjoyed an extraordinary rapport with his colleagues, both seniors and juniors. He has had high regard for those who took the time to mentor and guide him and has remained in touch with most of his former Ambassadors and superiors. He has had an extraordinary connection with External Affairs Minister Dr. S. Jaishankar. In fact, it was the External Affairs Minister who selected him prematurely for an appointment to one of the prestigious posts in the Indian Foreign Service as High Commissioner to Bangladesh. Shringla feels, and always felt fortunate, to work with a person of extraordinary calibre and experience as the current External Affairs Minister. Their working relationship has contributed to an exceptional phase of the Ministry of External Affair's performance in the larger government system.

Shringla was also highly regarded by Prime Minister Modi who called him to brief the Cabinet and Cabinet Committee on Security on a number of occasions, including on Afghanistan after the fall of Kabul to the Taliban, and Ukraine at the start of the conflict. Those who worked with Shringla recall his being called upon to make over a hundred presentations to the PM, many in areas Shringla did not directly deal with at the time, such as Central Asia, the UAE and Australia.

Harsh Shringla has equally benefited from his close engagement with all the younger officers and staff who came in contact with him. Always a team player, Shringla worked inclusively with all under his charge in organising any major event or activity. Taking the team along, and carrying his other colleagues with him, in a cooperative and inclusive manner has, in fact, been his forte. He recalls his work on concluding a security agreement with Myanmar about a decade ago in which he remembers working closely with his counterparts in the Ministry of Home Affairs, Defence, the Army and the agencies. He always ensured that his counterparts were an integral part of the negotiations with Myanmar. The result of this approach ensured that the draft Cabinet Note that led to the conclusion of the Agreement was approved by all the concerned Ministries in a record 24 hours.

In his current capacity, Shringla continues to work on this approach in a close and cooperative manner with all of his colleagues in keeping with the whole-of-government approach philosophy advocated by Prime Minister Narendra Modi, and working towards proactive and enduring Foreign Policy.

The last word has not been written about Harsh Shringla. He continues to serve his country with determination, grit and passion with a calm, composed mind filled with kindness and compassion in his heart to serve mankind to the best of his ability.

NOTES

1. H.V. Shringla, personal interview, February 5, 2022
2. S. Shringla, personal interview, September 17, 2021
3. N. Khadga, personal interview, September 20, 2021
4. D. Wangdi, personal interview, September 11, 2021
5. P. Basnet, personal communication, October 21, 2021
6. L. Puri, personal interview, September 16, 2021
7. A. Kabir, personal interview, September 10, 2021
8. S. Dorjee, personal interview, September 1, 2021
9. S. Lakshman, personal interview, January, 19, 2022
10. T. Lungri, personal interview, September 3, 2021
11. N. Panday, personal interview, September 9, 2021
12. A. Kabir, personal interview, September 7, 2021
13. A. Ray, personal interview, February 4, 2022
14. S. Kulkarni, personal interview, September 29, 2021

15. R. Bhatia, personal interview, September 29, 2021
16. A. Kumar, personal interview, September 28, 2021
17. A. Mubai, personal interview, September 20, 2021
18. N. Bhusan, personal interview, November 11, 2021
19. S. Panday, personal interview, October 1, 2021
20. S. P. Singh, personal interview, September 27, 2021
21. A. Mathur, personal interview, October 2. 2021
22. R. Pal, personal interview, September 9, 2021
23. S. Chakoborty, personal interview, September 2, 2021
24. R. Kumar, personal interview, November 23, 2021
25. Shayela, personal interview, September 28. 2021
26. T. Langry, personal interview, September 8, 2021

BIBLIOGRAPHY

1. The ICFAI University, Sikkim bestowed on him a DLitt Honoris Causa Honorary Doctorate degree on September 9, 2019 for mastering nuances of diplomacy and helping the reputation of his nation, at https://www.youtube.com/watch?v=FM0XBpEW4VI&t=92s. Accessed on June 22, 2021.
2. "NRC will not impact Bangladesh, Foreign Secretary Shringla tells Dhaka", at https://www.thehindu.com/news/international/nrc-wont-have-implications-on-bangladesh-says-foreign-secretary-shringla/article30962241.ece. Accessed on July 5, 2021.
3. Harsh Vardhan Shringla. "India is a constructive, dependable actor globally". *Hindustan Times*, at https://www.hindustantimes.com/analysis/india-is-a-constructive-dependable-actor-globally/story-QSoRIxr4QtmaDAIBAOCYuN.html. Accessed on July 6, 2021.

4. "Foreign Secretary Harsh Shringla Meets Bangladesh PM Hasina, Discusses Post-Covid Economic Recovery", at https://www.news18.com/news/india/in-second-visit-to-bangladesh-as-foreign-secretary-harsh-shringla-arrives-in-dhaka-2797681.html. Accessed on July 5, 2021.
5. "On 2 and 3 March, 2020 India's newly-appointed foreign secretary Harsh Vardhan Shringla visited Dhaka to prepare the grounds for Prime Minister Narendra Modi's now-cancelled visit to Dhaka on 17 March", at https://www.firstpost.com/india/foreign-secretary-harsh-v-shringlas-bangladesh-visit-represents-a-friends-assurance-to-dhaka-on-host-of-bilateral-matters-8143011.html. Accessed on July 5, 2020.
6. India-Bangladesh Joint Statement during Official Visit of Prime Minister of Bangladesh to India, October 5, 2019, at https://mea.gov.in/bilateral-documents.htm?dtl/31911/IndiaBangladesh_Joint_Statement_during_Official_Visit_of_Prime_Minister_of_Bangladesh_to_India. Accessed on August 14, 2020.
7. List of MoUs/Agreements exchanged during Official Visit of Prime Minister of Bangladesh to India, October 5, 2019, at https://mea.gov.in/bilateral-documents.htm?dtl/31910/List_of_MoUsAgreements_exchanged_during_Official_Visit_of_Prime_Minister_of_Bangladesh_to_India. Accessed on August 14, 2020.
8. Joint Press Release on Joint Consultative Commission between India and Bangladesh, February 8, 2019, at https://mea.gov.in/bilateraldocuments.htm?dtl/31015/Joint_Press_Release_on_Joint_Consultative_Commission_between_India_and_Bangladesh. Accessed on August 14, 2020.
9. List of MoUs signed during India-Bangladesh 5th JCC, February 8, 2019, at https://mea.gov.in/bilateraldocuments.htm?dtl/31016/List_of_MoUs_signed_during_India__Bangladesh_5th_JCC. Accessed on August 14, 2020.
10. India-Bangladesh Joint Statement during the State Visit of Prime Minister of Bangladesh to India, April 8, 2017, at URL: https://mea.gov.in/

bilateral-documents.htm?dtl/28362/India__Bangladesh_Joint_Statement_during_the_State_Visit_of_Prime_Minister_of_Bangladesh_to_India_April_8_2017. Accessed on August 14, 2020.

11. S. Res. 357—A resolution celebrating the 150th anniversary of the birth of Mahatma Gandhi. 116th Congress (2019-2020), at https://www.congress.gov/bill/116th-congress/senate-resolution/357/text. Accessed on August 23, 2020.
12. List of Agreements/MoUs exchanged during the State Visit of Prime Minister of Bangladesh to India, April 8, 2017, at https://mea.gov.in/bilateral-documents.htm?dtl/28360/List_of_AgreementsMoUs_exchanged_during_the_State_Visit_of_Prime_Minister_of_Bangladesh_to_India_April_0710_2017. Accessed on August 14, 2020.

Thailand 2014-2016

13. List of Agreements/MOUs signed during the Visit of Minister of External Affairs to Thailand, June 29, 2015, at https://mea.gov.in/bilateral-documents.htm?dtl/25412/List_of_AgreementsMOUs_signed_during_the_Visit_of_Minister_of_External_Affairs_to_Thailand_2729_June_2015. Accessed on August 28, 2020.
14. India-Thailand Joint Statement during the visit of Prime Minister of Thailand to India, June 17, 2016, at https://mea.gov.in/bilateral-documents.htm?dtl/26923/IndiaThailand_Joint_Statement_during_the_visit_of_Prime_Minister_of_Thailand_to_India. Accessed on August 28, 2020.

United States 2019-2020

15. India and United States Renew Triangular Development Cooperation in Asia and Africa, March 29, 2019, at https://mea.gov.in/bilateral-documents.htm?dtl/31189/India_and_United_States_Renew_Triangular_Development_Cooperation_in_Asia_and_Africa. Accessed on July 12, 2021.

2021

16. Foreign Secretary's Remarks at the World Health Organization's "South-East Asia Regional Health Partners' Forum on COVID-19", June 3, 2021, at https://mea.gov.in/Speeches-Statements.htm?dtl/33891/Foreign_Secretarys_Remarks_at_the_World_Health_Organizations_SouthEast_Asia_Regional_Health_Partners_Forum_on_COVID19_03_June_2021. Accessed on July 7, 2021.
17. Foreign Secretary's Remarks at the Release of Commemorative Postage Stamp on 70th anniversary of the Establishment of Diplomatic Relations between India and Germany, June 10, 2021, at https://mea.gov.in/Speeches-Statements.htm?dtl/33901/Foreign_Secretarys_Remarks_at_the_Release_of_Commemorative_Postage_Stamp_on_70th_anniversary_of_the_Establishment_of_Diplomatic_Relations_between_India. Accessed on July 7, 2021.
18. Statement by Foreign Secretary at UNSC high-level meeting on "Maintenance of international peace and security: upholding multilateralism and the United Nations-centered international system", May 7, 2021, at https://indianembassy-moscow.gov.in/press-releases-EAM-07-05-2021-1.php. Accessed on July 7, 2021.
19. Keynote Address by Foreign Secretary at the Inaugural Session of the International Relations Conference 2021 Organised by Symbiosis School of International Studies, at https://www.aninews.in/news/business/business/symbiosis-to-host-7th-edition-of-international-relations-conference20210428201250. Accessed on July 7, 2021.
20. Foreign Secretary's Address at Sikkim University, Gangtok, April 3, 2021, at www.mea.gov.in. Accessed on July 7, 2021.
21. Foreign Secretary's message at event to commemorate the 60th death anniversary of Shri K. Sankara Pillai, IFS, formerly First Secretary, High Commission of India, Ottawa, April 19, 2021, at www.mea.gov.in. Accessed on July 7, 2021.

22. Remarks by Foreign Secretary at the Ananta Aspen Centre on the Launch of the Paper on "India: The World's Pharmacy Expands Its Reach in Global Health", March 30, 2021, at www.mea.gov.in. Accessed on July 7, 2021.
23. Foreign Secretary's address at Ananta Aspen Centre on "What Next for Neighbourhood First", March 15, 2021, at www.mea.gov.in. Accessed on July 9, 2021.
24. Foreign Secretary's Remarks at the Inauguration of the South Asia Group on Energy at the Research and Information System for Developing Countries, March 10, 2021, at www.mea.gov.in. Accessed on July 12, 2021.
25. Foreign Secretary's Address at the Inaugural Session of the Dialogue on "Development of North Eastern Indian Region: Indo-Japan Collaboration for Connectivity, Commerce, Capacity Building, Culture and Conservation", March 5, 2021, at https://www.in.emb-japan.go.jp/itpr_en/11_000001_00137.html. Accessed on July 9, 2021.
26. Foreign Secretary's Statement at the High-Level Segment of the Conference on Disarmament, February 22, 2021, at mea.gov.in, Accessed on July 9, 2021.
27. Foreign Secretary's Lecture on "Expectations from India in the Emerging World Order Post COVID-19", Haryana Institute of Public Administration. February 22, 2021, at www.mea.gov.in. Accessed on July 9, 2021.
28. Foreign Secretary's Speech at the Russian Diplomatic Academy, Moscow. At URL: Foreign Secretary's Speech at the Russian Diplomatic Academy, Moscow, February 17, 2021, www.mea.gov.in. Accessed on July 9, 2021.
29. Foreign Secretary's Remarks at the Inaugural Function of the 3rd Bangladesh Film Festival, Kolkata, February 5, 2021, at www.mea.gov.in Accessed on July 9, 2021.
30. Foreign Secretary's Introductory Remarks at the India-France-Japan Workshop on the Indo-Pacific, January 19, 2021, at www.mea.gov.in Accessed on July 9, 2021.
31. Remarks by the Foreign Secretary at the Signing Ceremony of the Memorandum of Cooperation on Specified Skilled Workers with Japan, January 18, 2021, at www.mea.gov.in. Accessed on July 9, 2021.

32. Remarks by Shri Harsh Vardhan Shringla, Foreign Secretary at the UN Security Council Open Debate, "Challenges of maintaining peace and security in fragile contexts", January 6, 2021, at mea.gov.in. Accessed on July 9, 2021.

2020

33. Virtual Address by Foreign Secretary at the Inaugural Session of the North East Festival, December 19, 2020, at mea.gov.in. Accessed on July 9, 2021.
34. Foreign Secretary's Remarks at the "Global Heritage Series". Organised by SPIC MACAY, December 6, 2020, at mea.gov.in. Accessed on July 9, 2021.
35. Opening Statement by the Foreign Secretary at the Indo-German 1.5 Track Dialogue, 2020, November 27, 2020, at mea.gov.in. Accessed on July 9, 2021.
36. Address by Foreign Secretary at AIDIA Distinguished Lecture, November 27, 2020, at mea.gov.in. Accessed on July 9, 2021.
37. Foreign Secretary's Remarks at the Third Permanent Court of Arbitration (PCA)—India Conference, November 21, 2020, at mea.gov.in. Accessed on July 9, 2021.
38. Foreign Secretary's Remarks at the Virtual Interaction with the US India Strategic Partnership Forum, November 19, 2020, at mea.gov.in. Accessed on July 9, 2021.
39. Foreign Secretary's Remarks at the Handing Over of Children's Parks for 67 Islands in Maldives under Cash Grant Projects, National Stadium, Malé, November 9, 2020, at mea.gov.in. Accessed on July 9, 2021.
40. Foreign Secretary's Remarks at the Ministry of Foreign Affairs, Government of Maldives, November 9, 2020, at mea.gov.in. Accessed on July 9, 2021.
41. Foreign Secretary's remarks at briefing session on COVID-19 related issues for diplomatic missions and international organisations, November 6, 2020, at mea.gov.in. Accessed on July 9, 2021.

42. Foreign Secretary's Address on "Leveraging Strategic Autonomy in a Turbulent World" at the Diamond Jubilee Seminar of the National Defence College, November 5, 2020, at mea.gov.in. Accessed on July 9, 2021.
43. Foreign Secretary's Speech at Policy Exchange, November 3, 2020, at mea.gov.in. Accessed on July 9, 2021.
44. Foreign Secretary's Remarks at Institut Français des Relations Internationales (IFRI), Paris on "India's Foreign Policy in the Post-Covid World" October 29, 2020, at mea.gov.in. Accessed on July 9, 2021.
45. Message from Foreign Secretary on the Day of Languages Celebrated by Mayo College, Ajmer and Goethe Institute, October 26, 2020, at mea.gov.in. Accessed on July 9, 2021.
46. Foreign Secretary's Virtual Keynote Address at the Inaugural Session of the Course on "India and the Reshaping of the World Order", St. Stephen's College, September 21, 2020, at mea.gov.in. Accessed on July 9, 2021.
47. Virtual Address by the Foreign Secretary at CII's Annual Conference in the UK, September 15, 2020, at mea.gov.in. Accessed on July 9, 2021.
48. Remarks by Foreign Secretary on the "Impact of Neighbourhood First and Act East Policies on the North East", September 10, 2020, at mea.gov.in. Accessed on July 9, 2021.
49. Foreign Secretary's Virtual Address to ICAI on Implementing the Vision of Aatmanirbhar Bharat, July 6, 2020, at mea.gov.in. Accessed on July 9, 2021.
50. Foreign Secretary's address on "New World Order Post COVID-19" to the Federation of Indian Chambers of Commerce & Industry (FICCI), May 20, 2020, at mea.gov.in. Accessed on July 9, 2021.
51. Foreign Secretary's Virtual Address to the National Defence College on "India's Foreign Policy Options in the Emerging World Order", May 15, 2020, at mea.gov.in. Accessed on July 9, 2021.
52. Foreign Secretary's Virtual Address to MIT World Peace University, Pune on the Importance of Multilateralism in the Time of a Global Pandemic—An Indian Perspective, May 11, 2020, at mea.gov.in. Accessed on July 9, 2021.

53. Foreign Secretary's Speech at Bangladesh Institute for International Strategic Studies (BIISS) Event, March 2, 2020, at mea.gov.in. Accessed on July 9, 2021.
54. Foreign Secretary's Speech at the Valedictory Session of the Conference "Understanding Africa: Continuity and Change" at the India International Centre, February 12, 2020, at mea.gov.in. Accessed on July 9, 2021.
55. Remarks by Foreign Secretary on the 70th Anniversary Celebration of the Fulbright Program in India, February 4, 2020, at mea.gov.in. Accessed on July 9, 2021.
56. Media statement by Shri Harsh Vardhan Shringla on assuming charge as Foreign Secretary, January 29, 2020, at mea.gov.in. Accessed on July 9, 2021.

MEA Annual Reports

57. 1991-2001, Annual Report, MEA, Patiala House Library. New Delhi.
58. 2002-2008, Annual Report, MEA, Patiala House Library. New Delhi.
59. Annual Report, 2021-2022, MEA, at https://www.mea.gov.in/Uploads/PublicationDocs/34894_MEA_Annual_Report_English.pdf. Accessed on December 3, 2022.
60. Annual Report, 2020-2021, MEA, at https://www.mea.gov.in/Uploads/PublicationDocs/33569_MEA_annual_Report.pdf. Accessed on December 3, 2022.
61. Annual Report, 2019-2020, MEA, at https://www.mea.gov.in/Uploads/PublicationDocs/32489_AR_Spread_2020_new.pdf. Accessed on October 13, 2021.
62. Annual Report, 2018-2019, MEA, at https://main.mohfw.gov.in/basicpage/annual-report-2018-19. Accessed on October 13, 2021.
63. Annual Report, 2017-2018, MEA, at https://dpiit.gov.in/anual-report/annual-report-2017-18. Accessed on October 13, 2021.
64. Annual Report, 2016-2017, MEA, at https://dpiit.gov.in/anual-report/annual-report-2016-17. Accessed on October 13, 2021.

65. Annual Report, 2015-2016, MEA, at https://www.mea.gov.in/images/ris_2015_2016.pdf. Accessed on October 14, 2021.
66. Annual Report, 2014-2015, MEA, at https://www.mea.gov.in/Uploads/PublicationDocs/25009_External_Affairs_2014-2015__English_.pdf Accessed on October 14, 2021.
67. Annual Report, 2013-2014, MEA, at https://www.mea.gov.in/Uploads/PublicationDocs/23873_EXTERNAL_AFFAIR__Eng__AR_2013-14.pdf. Accessed on October 14, 2021.
68. Annual Report, 2012-2013, MEA, at https://www.mea.gov.in/Uploads/PublicationDocs/21385_Annual_Report_2012-2013_English.pdf. Accessed on October 14, 2021.
69. Annual Report, 2011-2012, MEA, at https://www.mea.gov.in/Uploads/PublicationDocs/19337_annual-report-2011-2012.pdf. Accessed on October 14, 2021.
70. Annual Report, 2010-2011, MEA, at https://www.mea.gov.in/Uploads/PublicationDocs/45_Annual-Report-2010-2011.pdf. Accessed on October 14, 2021.
71. Annual Report, 2009-2010, MEA, at https://www.mea.gov.in/Uploads/PublicationDocs/171_Annual-Report-2009-2010.pdf. Accessed on October 14, 2021.

INDEX